CW00920181

OLD TES

*General Editor*

R.N. Whybray

# JUDGES

# JUDGES

## A.D.H. Mayes

Published by JSOT Press
for the Society for Old Testament Study

First published by JSOT Press 1985
Reprinted 1989

Copyright © 1985, 1989 Sheffield Academic Press

Published by JSOT Press
JSOT Press is an imprint of
Sheffield Academic Press Ltd
The University of Sheffield
343 Fulwood Road
Sheffield S10 3BP
England

Printed and bound in Great Britain
by Dotesios (Printers) Ltd.,
Bradford-on-Avon, Wiltshire.


British Library Cataloguing in Publication Data

[Bible. O.T. Judges. *English* 1985]. Judges.—
(Old Testament guides, ISSN 0264-6498; 3)
1. Bible. O.T. Judges—Criticism, interpretation, etc.
I. Title      II. Mayes, A.D.H.      III. Series
222'.3206      BS1305.2

ISBN 0-905774-58-2

# CONTENTS

## Preface

Much of the work on this volume was done during a period of seven months which I was privileged to spend at the University of Tübingen in 1983. That visit was made possible by the generous support of the Alexander von Humboldt-Stiftung and by the warm welcome and thoughtful hospitality of Professor Martin Hengel. I am glad now to have the opportunity to record my appreciation both to that foundation and to Professor Hengel; their generosity made an academic visit into an enriching and rewarding experience for me and my family.

I am indebted also to Professor R.N. Whybray, both for his invitation to contribute to the series 'Old Testament Guides' and for his advice and helpful comments while the work was in progress. As always, however, the real stresses and strains of writing have been borne by my wife, Elizabeth; my gratitude for that cannot adequately be expressed here.

A.D.H. Mayes
Trinity College, Dublin

# Abbreviations

| | |
|---|---|
| ATANT | Abhandlungen zur Theologie des Alten und Neuen Testaments |
| BA | *Biblical Archaeologist* |
| BASOR | *Bulletin of the American Schools of Oriental Research* |
| BBB | Bonner Biblische Beiträge |
| Bib | *Biblica* |
| BWANT | Beiträge zur Wissenschaft vom Alten und Neuen Testament |
| BZ | *Biblische Zeitschrift* |
| BZAW | Beihefte zur *Zeitschrift für die alttestamentliche Wissenschaft* |
| CBQ | *Catholic Biblical Quarterly* |
| HTR | *Harvard Theological Review* |
| HUCA | *Hebrew Union College Annual* |
| IDBSup | *Interpreter's Dictionary of the Bible*, Supplementary Volume |
| IEJ | *Israel Exploration Journal* |
| JBL | *Journal of Biblical Literature* |
| JNES | *Journal of Near Eastern Studies* |
| JSOT | *Journal for the Study of the Old Testament* |
| JTS | *Journal of Theological Studies* |
| PEQ | *Palestine Exploration Quarterly* |
| RB | *Revue biblique* |
| SBL | Society of Biblical Literature |
| TLZ | *Theologische Literaturzeitung* |
| UF | *Ugarit-Forschungen* |
| VT | *Vetus Testamentum* |
| VTS | Supplement to *Vetus Testamentum* |
| WMANT | Wissenschaftliche Monographien zum Alten und Neuen Testament |
| ZAW | *Zeitschrift für die alttestamentliche Wissenschaft* |

# 1

## THE BOOK OF JUDGES

### A. The Writing of History in the Book of Judges

THE FIRST concerns of a historian are with the identification and right evaluation of his sources. However, his decisions on these issues are inevitably going to be influenced both by the particular questions which he consciously brings to his subject, and also by the presuppositions which are part of his unconscious make-up; and to that extent it must be admitted that his results cannot be described as purely objective history. On the other hand, this recognition cannot possibly justify any and every interpretation or historical reconstruction: the sources do impose external constraints and our use of them is an activity in which the questions we ask and the results we achieve are constantly guided and informed by the material available. What this means in effect is that the history we write is a story; it is a story for our time which is as thoroughly as possible built upon and derived from the oldest and most reliable materials available on the subject. It has as its object and purpose the making meaningful of the past for the present.

These considerations are by no means irrelevant to our present context, for it is perfectly clear that the writing of history in the way described is an activity which lies behind much of the Old Testament itself, including the book of Judges, and so, in a certain sense, our concerns here represent the concerns also of some Old Testament writers. They too are making the past meaningful for the present; they too use older sources to achieve their purpose; however, their use of those sources is guided not just by the sources themselves but by the conscious and unconscious presuppositions and questions with which they approach their subject. Their presuppositions and methods and ours are, of course, far from identical: their intention is much more deliberately didactic than historical, and they often simply include sources within a framework commentary rather than use them as a basis for writing a new history. However, both then and now it is an interpretative function in which the authors are engaged.

This constitutes a basic and important starting point for our discussion of the book of Judges. The history of Israel in the period of the judges which is related there is an account with a clearly didactic purpose, or, rather, given the complexity of the book, a number of clearly didactic purposes. The time of the last writer at work is far removed from that of the earlier authors who composed the sources which have been later used, and the use to which those sources have been put amounts to an interpretation appropriate to the time at which that last writer worked. This does not imply, of course, that in order to recover the real history one must simply discard the later interpretation which appears in the framework surrounding the older sources; those older sources are themselves stories about events and so, therefore, interpretations of events, in the period of the judges. Ultimately the events are there, but the attempt to understand them and set them in meaningful connections and contexts starts right with the events themselves. The origin of the book of Judges is, therefore, an interpretative process in which the past is being continuously related to an ever-changing present. It is that process which we today, with our very different presuppositions, questions and methods of inquiry, have inherited.

## B. The Deuteronomistic Context of the Book of Judges

The book of Judges is the third book of an account of Israel's history which starts at the beginning of Deuteronomy and goes on to the end of the second book of Kings. We owe the classic study of this history to Martin Noth who first presented a persuasive case for treating this part of the Old Testament as a single literary unit, to be called the deuteronomistic history. That designation reflects the dependence of the work, both for its language and its theology, on the first book which it includes, Deuteronomy. It is the deuteronomic law which the deuteronomistic historian has taken up at the beginning of his work, provided with a historical framework, and used as a basic guide by which to present an account of the history of Israel leading up to his own time.

Four features in particular of this historical work indicate that it is such a unity. First, the language of the work shows a certain consistency pointing to unity of authorship: it is plain, lacking 'any particular artistry or refinement', and it is notably repetitive. Secondly, there appear at decisive points through the work speeches or narratives, all of which share not only this deuteronomistic style of writing but also a common function and purpose: they are designed to review the course of the history which has just passed and to derive from that history moral and theological lessons for the future. These deuteronomistic compositions, which bind the whole work together into a single unit, are to be found in Josh. 1, set on the eve of Israel's entry into the land; Josh. 12, marking the completion of the conquest of the land; Josh. 23, cast as Joshua's farewell speech and admonition to Israel for its future life in the land; Judg. 2.11ff., inaugurating the period of the judges; 1 Sam. 12, in which Samuel's farewell speech marks the conclusion of the period of the judges and the opening of the monarchic period; 1 Kings 8.14ff., being Solomon's prayer of dedication of the temple; 2 Kings 17.7ff., which comprises a reflection on the disastrous history of the monarchic period. Thirdly, there is a consistent chronology throughout the work. There are problems involved in harmonizing the various chronological statements, but these arise either from later insertions in the history or from our misunderstanding the intention of the deuteronomist; there does exist a basic uniform chronology which holds the whole history together. Fourthly, there is a theological unity which is manifest especially in the consistency with which an overall theme is maintained. This theme is the history of Israel as something completed and past: it was a history of disobedience to the covenant law as a result of which Israel had to suffer the consequences of the curse attached to that covenant law; breach of covenant had brought the covenant relationship with Yahweh to an end, and so Israel had reached the end of its history. The deuteronomistic historian has no concern with a future for Israel; such a future does not exist.

The deuteronomistic history, composed after the destruction of Judah and Jerusalem in 587 BC, is the first presentation of the history of Israel. It is the creative and original work of an author, not just the editing of an already existing account. The deuteronomist was an author who made use of a variety of sources in order to create something new. He was selective and systematic: selective in that, as one can see especially from his referring the reader of Kings elsewhere for further information (1 Kings 11.41; etc.), he did not incorporate everything available to him; systematic in that he has organized his sources in order to present the history of Israel in four major periods, that of Moses, that of the conquest, that of the judges and that of the monarchy. The period of the judges begins with the preview now found in Judg. 2.11ff., and is brought to an end with the speech of Samuel in 1 Sam. 12.

Noth's view has stood the test of time, despite the assaults which have been made on it. Attempts to distinguish pre-deuteronomistic continuous sources within the deuteronomistic history, in Joshua, Joshua to Judges, or even into Samuel and Kings, and so to weaken the presentation of the deuteronomist as Israel's first historian have not been successful; parallel sources, whether or not to be seen as continuations of the Pentateuchal sources, cannot be satisfactorily uncovered. On the other hand, the attempt of Fohrer and others to demonstrate the lack of unity in the deuteronomistic history by arguing that different deuteronomistic hands have at different times edited the various books comprising the deuteronomistic history, has been no more successful. There are indeed differences, as von Rad has shown, in the understanding of the nature of history in different parts of the deuteronomistic history. Thus, the book of Judges is dominated by a presentation of history as a recurrent cycle of typical occurrences, while in Kings history is understood in linear terms as a time of increasing sin and turning away from Yahweh until at last he destroys Israel. This difference is a striking one, but one must weigh against it the clear indications of unity in the history which prohibit any such division between the various books; and this in turn suggests the possibility that where differences exist they belong to different levels within what must in general terms continue to be seen as a uniform and single work. In other words, the cyclic pattern of presentation of history in Judges is a fundamental characteristic of a stage of development of that book which is not to be set on the same level as the linear presentation of history in Kings.

This approach, which acknowledges both the diversity and the unity within the work, is supported by one fairly major modification of Noth's work which does seem to be required: it is likely that Noth underestimated the extent to which the deuteronomistic history was at a later stage edited to give it a quite new slant for a new situation. Thus, it appears that the original deuteronomistic history was a work composed in the first instance in pre-exilic times, in the light of and as support for a reform carried out by the Judean king Josiah. The work was concerned especially to emphasize the unity of Israel under one leader—Moses, David and Josiah being the three key figures. However, after the destruction of Judah and the exile this work was edited, not only by extending the limits of the history up to the destruction, but by introducing much new material in order to give the history its present negative and pessimistic tone. Although a hint of a promise for a better future is present, the work became essentially an address to the exiles summoning them to a recognition of the reasons for their plight and calling them to repentance. Even this, however, did not mark the final completion of the editorial work on the history: further additions were made, of isolated material, some of it, apparently, deriving from quite ancient times. In all of these respects the book of Judges shows a picture consistent with the rest of the deuteronomistic history.

## C. The Structure of the Book of Judges

The book falls into three quite clearly defined sections: a prologue in Judg. 1.1–2.5 and an epilogue in chs. 17–21 introduce and conclude the central substance of the book in Judg. 2.6–16.31. They are distinct from the central section in a number of respects: they do not describe any great act of deliverance wrought by a judge or deliverer raised up by Yahweh; they are not concerned with relations between Israel and non-Israelites outside its land; they emphasize internal disunity within the people, both military and moral. It is only in the central part, in Judg. 2.6–16.31, that we have a history of Israel in the period of the judges.

### a. The prologue and epilogue

The distinction between prologue and epilogue, on the one hand, and the central section, on the other hand, is probably to be seen as a result of the history of development of the book, the prologue and epilogue deriving from a hand different from that responsible for the central history; and since it can be demonstrated that the prologue and epilogue are intrusions into a continuous account which relates Joshua to Judges and Judges to Samuel, it may be concluded that the prologue and epilogue are, from a redactional point of view, later than the central section of the book.

Josh. 24.29-30 brings the deuteronomistic book of Joshua to a close with a note on the death and burial of Joshua. The substance of this report appears again in Judg. 2.6-10 where it is, however, considerably more elaborate. It is now not just the death of Joshua which is marked, but also that of the whole generation of Joshua which had had immediate experience of the work of Yahweh in Israel's history. There is certainly a literary relationship between the two passages, though the nature of that relationship has been the subject of some discussion. Josh. 24.29-30 has sometimes been seen as secondary in relation to Judg. 2.6-10, inserted in order to mark off the book of Joshua as a quite independent literary entity; however, it seems best to take the opposite view and to understand that the longer, more elaborate and more theologically developed account in Judg. 2.6-10 is later than and built on the shorter and more historically informative account in Josh. 24.29-30. That historical note has been taken up again in Judg. 2.6-10 as a result of the secondary incorporation of the material in Judg. 1.1–2.5; this secondary material disrupted the original continuity of the account which ran from the death of Joshua into the account of the period of the judges now contained within Judg. 2.11–16.31. Thus, the prologue to the book of Judges in 1.1–2.5 must be an addition to the originally continuous deuteronomistic history.

The epilogue in Judg. 17–21 is a similar interruption. These five chapters relate two different stories, and of these at least the second is also composite; but certain common features hold them together as one literary unit. They are accounts of events involving a Levite from Judah, and are set in a time when 'there was no king in Israel; every man did what was right in his own eyes' (Judg. 17.6; 21.25; cf. also 18.1; 19.1). The independence of the unit as a whole from the central part of the book is indicated by the fact that the subjects it covers are without parallel in Judg. 2.11–16.31, while the theme of the latter, Israel's deliverance from the oppression of external enemies, does not feature in the epilogue. Furthermore, there is a fairly strong element of continuity between the Jephthah and Samson stories of Judg. 10–16 and the beginning of the books of Samuel. So, Judg. 10.7 relates that Israel was sold by Yahweh into the power of the Philistines and Ammonities; the threat of Ammonites is the background for the immediately following story of Jephthah, and the threat of the Philistines lies behind not only the story of Samson but also that of Samuel in 1 Sam. 4–7. Secondly, the chronological statement of Judg. 13.1, that Yahweh gave Israel into the hand of the Philistines for forty years, refers to the period covered by the Samson and Samuel stories, but bears no relation to the events narrated in Judg. 17–21. Thus, Judg. 17–21, like the prologue in Judg. 1.1–2.5, disrupt the continuity of the deuteronomistic history.

This treatment of the prologue and epilogue is confirmed by the fact that they share several features which do not characterize Judg. 2.11–16.31; and these features not only indicate their independence of the central section, but also show that the prologue and epilogue have probably come into their present position as the result of the same post-deuteronomistic editing. In both sections it is inner Israelite moral and spiritual degeneration which is prominent; cultic lamentation and sacrifice also feature in both (Judg. 2.4f.; 20.23, 26). It also seems likely that both, whatever may be their actual historical value, represent basically monarchic propaganda deriving from a time, perhaps early in the monarchic period, when opposition to the monarchy was strong. This is the case quite explicitly in Judg. 17–21 which deliberately set out to portray Israel without the monarchy as a time when only the law of the strongest ruled. It is the anarchy of Israel without the monarchy which justifies and supports the monarchy.

Somewhat less clearly is this pro-monarchic attitude also to be found in Judg. 1. This chapter has frequently been highly valued as a source of reliable historical information. Although introduced in v. 1 as an account of events after the death of Joshua, it has usually been treated as a record of Israel's actual settlement of the land, parallel to, and yet much more trustworthy than, that contained in the book of Joshua. It depicts the Israelite tribes acting more or less independently to secure their territory and is frank in its admission that much of the land west of the Jordan remained free of Israelite control. In both respects it has been thought to be free of the idealization of the book of Joshua, and so to be much closer to the event of Israel's settlement as it actually occurred. It is easy, however, to exaggerate this aspect of the nature of Judg. 1. An interest in history for its own sake is not exactly characteristic of the Old Testament, and it would be strange to find it here. If one asks whose interests are being served by Judg. 1, particularly by the features of the chapter we have highlighted, a conclusion emerges which suggests that the chapter is a story told with a very definite intention and audience in view. Through emphasizing the disunity of Israel and its failure to secure the land in the pre-monarchic period, Judg. 1 intends to highlight the need for strong and united leadership as provided by the monarchy, through which the land is secured. This is an account which in fact vindicates the monarchy, and especially the monarchy of David and Solomon, under whom those areas which the tribes could not conquer were incorporated into Israel.

In the cases of both prologue and epilogue in Judges we have, therefore, records of indeterminate origin, but records which seem fundamentally to be concerned with upholding the monarchic state. They have been brought very late into their present position, at a time after the composition of the deuteronomistic history the continuity of which they disrupt. The intention of the editor who incorporated them is not clear: it need not have been identical with the original pro-monarchic concerns of the records; indeed, it may be that this late editor simply saw in them useful illustrations of the moral and spiritual state of Israel in this period, which he could use to mark off the book of Judges as a separate literary entity. In addition, Judg. 1 provided the historical reason for the situation, presupposed in Judg. 2.11ff., that Canaanites still remained in the land given to Israel by Yahweh.

### b. The nature of the central section

The central section of Judges, in Judg. 2.11–16.31, contains the deuteronomistic account of the period of the judges. It is not the complete deuteronomistic account of this period, for it is clear from the speeches in Josh. 23 and 1 Sam. 12, which are used as structural markers in the deuteronomistic history, that while the introduction to this period lies in Judg. 2.11ff., its conclusion is not reached until the inauguration of the monarchy under Saul in 1 Sam. 8–12. It is as a result of post-deuteronomistic developments, in particular the introduction of Judg. 17–21, that the literary entity of the book of Judges has been established independently of the deuteronomistic literary unit devoted to that period. Yet, for our present purpose of understanding the origin and development of the book of Judges, we may confine our discussion to the central section of the book without risk of distortion.

Judg. 2.11–16.31 offers first a theological introduction to the period in 2.11–3.6; this is followed by accounts of concrete events and references to particular individuals. We may broadly distinguish between two categories of material and two types of individual: on the one hand, there are the stories of deliverers who were raised up by Yahweh to meet particular emergencies in which they delivered

Israel from oppression; on the other hand, there is in Judg. 10.1-5 and 12.7-15 the record of six individuals who are said to have judged Israel. About these, there is normally nothing related apart from the name, place of origin, period of time spent as judge, death and burial; it is a coherent and uniform list which stands independent of the stories of the deliverers. It is clearly a single list which has been secondarily divided; each judge is presented in a consistent and uniform way, and is directly connected with his predecessor by the words 'after him'. The one link between the list on the one hand and the stories of the deliverers on the other is formed by Jephthah, for he is not only a judge of the list (Judg. 12.7), but of him there also existed a story of his having delivered Israel (Judg. 10.6–12.6); it is that link which provided the basis and opportunity for the bringing together of these otherwise quite independent literary records. None of the other judges delivered Israel, nor did any of the other deliverers act as judge in the sense presupposed by the list of these judges. Whether we understand the verb 'judge' in a strictly judicial sense or, as is certainly possible, in the wider sense of 'rule' or 'govern', the difference between these two types of individual is clear: the deliverer is raised up by Yahweh to lead Israel in a specific emergency, and after coping with it he disappears from our view; the judge is the occupant of an office which was clearly not limited to a specific time of emergency but endured for the lifetime of its occupant. Jephthah was an exception, for, apparently (if we accept as historical the order in which events are presented) on the basis of the leadership which he displayed during the Ammonite emergency, he was made judge. However, there is no basis for assuming that a similar connection of roles existed also for the other deliverers and judges. These are essentially two different forms of literary record and two different types of individual, and it is only the fact that Jephthah alone happened to appear in both literary forms and among both types of individual which allowed the bringing together of the literary records in the way in which they now appear.

A preliminary conclusion may, therefore, be established: the central section of Judges is essentially composed of two different literary sources which have been brought together at a secondary stage of their development. The intended effect of this combination was to bring together both types of individual, so that in the period of the judges Israel could be presented as having been ruled by a succession of judge-deliverers. This intention is made explicit in the introduction given in Judg. 2.11–3.6 which describes the period of the judges as one in which Israel constantly sinned against Yahweh, was then sold into the power of enemies as punishment, and was then delivered by 'judges who saved them out of the power of those who plundered them' (2.16).

This provides a valid framework of understanding; we must now, however, refine it further in order to cater for various anomalies. In the following discussion our chief concern will be with the stories of deliverers, for it is this category which has been most extensively developed, first through the supplementation of a basic collection of deliverer stories, secondly, through the incorporation of the list of judges now to be found in Judg. 10.1-5 and 12.7-15, and, thirdly, through the provision of introductory material which is influenced by that integration of two different literary sources.

### c. The development of the central section

The major work on this topic has been carried out by W. Richter. This has shown that the history of development of the central section of the book of Judges may be discerned in all its considerable complexity by a study of the literary framework within which each of the stories of the deliverers is now included. The framework is complete and uniform with some of the stories, but appears only defectively with others, and it is this variation which allows us to determine the history of development of the central core of the book.

The literary framework consists of six elements. First, there is the declaration that 'Israel did what was evil'. This element is invariable in form and expression and appears in 2.11; 3.7, 12; 4.1; 6.1; 10.6; 13.1. Secondly, it is noted that Israel was delivered over to an enemy. There is some variation in expression here: 'the Lord sold them into the hand of . . .' (2.14; 3.8; 4.2; 10.7); 'the Lord strengthened . . . against Israel' (3.12); 'the Lord gave them into the hand of . . .' (6.1; 13.1). However, this element always amounts to a description of the military defeat of Israel by an enemy. Thirdly, it is reported that 'Israel cried to Yahweh' from their oppression (3.9, 15; 4.3; 6.6; 10.10). Fourthly, there appears the occasional statement that Yahweh 'raised up a deliverer' (3.9, 15). This element is so infrequent, however, that it should perhaps not be considered an independent constituent of the framework. It may represent a subordinate aspect of the third and fifth elements: although a deliverer is raised up in response to the cry of the people, it is Yahweh and not the deliverer who is the real leader and victor in the war with the enemy. The fifth element is the declaration that the enemy 'was subdued' (3.30; 8.28; 11.33); or 'God subdued . . . ' (4.23). Finally, it is stated that 'the land had rest' (3.11, 30; 5.31; 8.28).

This framework is not complete and consistent with all the stories in Judg. 2.11–16.31. Only the Ehud story in Judg. 3.12-30 exhibits all six elements; however, as noted above, the fourth element is probably not an essential constituent of the framework, and without this element the framework appears complete also with the stories of Deborah and Barak in Judg. 4–5 and of Gideon in Judg. 6–8. To these one should add the Abimelech story of Judg. 9, for this is too closely associated with the Gideon story to be taken as a very late addition to it; and in any case, since it is not a story of delivering Israel, it could not have been supplied with the framework which is typical of the Ehud, Deborah–Barak and Gideon collection. The basic collection of stories within the book of Judges comprises, therefore, the stories of Ehud, Deborah–Barak and Gideon–Abimelech.

The framework which characterizes this collection is quite clearly independent of and secondary to the stories it contains. Its language and style do not appear in the actual stories, and, whereas the stories relate the exploits of individuals and tribes against enemies, the framework introduces the quite new idea that it was the sin of the people which brought about the very conditions which made those exploits necessary. The framework represents, therefore, a particular stage in the history of the stories at which they have been made to serve a clear theological purpose. It is, however, only this purpose which the framework serves; it does not of itself hold the stories together as a collection. Rather, the stories already before the addition of the framework existed as a single collection. They all have a common interest in and reference to Israel; they are all concerned to present the events in which the deliverers were involved as holy wars in which Yahweh delivered his people.

There exists a certain tension between the interests of the pre-framework collection on the one hand and the actual traditions taken up into that collection on the other, for these traditions are focused on individual tribes or small groups of tribes rather than on Israel, and on the heroic exploits of individuals rather than on Yahweh's leadership of Israel in the holy war. Thus, it is clear that the oldest traditional material in the deliverer stories has undergone a number of transformations before reaching us. The two that have so far been identified are, first, the stage of being brought into a collection which introduced the all-Israel and holy war perspectives, and secondly, the stage of being supplied with a framework which set the stories in the context of sin against Yahweh and Yahweh's punishment and subsequent deliverance.

### i. *The basic collection of deliverer stories*
The first story of the collection (Judg. 3.12-30), relating Ehud's deliverance of Israel from the Moabites, offers a good illustration of the history of development which these stories have experienced. It is possible without much difficulty to recognize the essence of this story within vv. 15-25. It is a hero story, concentrating on the two figures, Ehud and Eglon. It provides no narrative background or context, but only those essential details which contribute most to the action of the story and the delineation of its central characters: Ehud the brave and cunning warrior of the clan of Gera in Benjamin, and Eglon, the fat and stupid king of Moab; Ehud the left-handed man with his sword secretly bound to his right thigh where its presence would not be suspected, and Eglon who is so fat that the sword sinks right into him, and whose nature is such that when he has been murdered Ehud has time to escape because the king's servants assume that the long-locked door means only the king is relieving himself in a leisurely fashion. This is a good and entertaining story, intended both to praise a local hero and to scorn a despised enemy. It was probably only at a secondary stage of its development that its scope was extended so that it became a story of a holy war between Israel and the Moabites, in which Yahweh raised up a deliverer and thousands of fleeing Moabites were killed by warriors of Ephraim and Benjamin (vv. 15, 27-29). Even this first adaptation of the story has shifted its primary focus away from the heroic exploit of the individual Ehud to Yahweh who through Ehud works deliverance for his people.

It is the introduction of the framework which has created the most decisive change in the story. It is no longer primarily a saving event of Yahweh which is related; rather, it is an act of mercy in which Yahweh delivers Israel from the results of its own sin. The Moabite king is no longer just a foe to be scorned, he is the divinely appointed instrument of Yahweh's punishment of his people Israel. Moreover, it is no longer just a story told for itself, but rather now an episode in a succession of such failures when Israel was repeatedly punished and then delivered. The original lively and to some extent coarse humour of the story, which so firmly anchored it in the everyday life of these ordinary people, is almost overcome by a deep seriousness which has a background and setting very different to that of the original context of popular story-telling.

The story in Judg. 4–5 of the victory of Israel led by Deborah and Barak over the kings of Canaan led by Sisera, presents a picture generally similar to that of the Ehud story: here too the framework has been added after the material had already reached an advanced stage of development. The situation here, however, is more complex, mainly because the account of the victory over Sisera exists in two versions, a prose account in Judg. 4 and a poem in Judg. 5. These differ from each other in some detail, but it is clear in any case that they cannot be treated together simply as constituent elements of one account. In one case there is a prose story, in the other a poem; these different literary forms point to different settings and a different literary history. They must, therefore, be examined independently in order to determine their origin and early development.

Judg. 4 is a story which falls into three paragraphs, each with different emphases and concerns: in vv. 1-11 the protagonists are introduced, Jabin the king of Canaan with his army commander Sisera on the one hand, Deborah the prophetess with Barak the army commander on the the other; in vv. 12-16 there is a formal account of the battle between the two sides, which comes to a quite clear conclusion; in vv. 17-22 we are given a detailed account of a particular event involving two single actors, Sisera and Jael. These are not only presentations of three consecutive stages in one event. There are substantial differences between the paragrpahs in substance and purpose, and these suggest a much more complex development in the course of which an old story has been given a historical setting and a theological interpretation.

In the first part of the story the reference to Jabin king of Canaan reigning at Hazor creates difficulties: the political unity and independence of Canaan, presupposed in the title 'king of Canaan', existed only under David and Solomon (who are, however, themselves never referred to as kings of Canaan); Jabin in this story otherwise plays no role, and is not referred to in Judg. 5. Where Jabin does feature, and in a more reliable context, is in Josh. 11.1-15, according to which he was defeated by Israel under Joshua at the time of the conquest. To that story probably belong both Jabin and the specific reference to Zebulun and Naphtali in Judg. 4.1-11. These tribes are not otherwise singled out, while their involvement in action against Hazor (Josh. 11) would, geographically, be much more credible. Two traditions, the destruction of Hazor and the defeat of Sisera, have been confused in Judg. 4.1-11. The confusion was caused by a number of factors: both traditions may have been transmitted at Tabor, a mountain sanctuary central to Judg. 4 (vv. 6, 12) and lying on the border of Zebulun and Naphtali; in both events Zebulun and Naphtali were involved; both events were of significance in terms of Israel's gaining control of the land, in the one case of the mountain area, in the other of the adjoining plain. Jabin, who appears again in vv. 17b, 23-24, may, therefore, be seen as a secondary accretion to the tradition of Judg. 4.

The account of Judg. 4.12-16 is a rather lifeless and stereotyped battle story. The only circumstantial detail appears in v. 15b with the information that Sisera fled away on foot; but this is quite clearly an additional note intended to link this paragraph with what follows in vv. 17-22. This middle section is in fact concerned with putting forward certain theological ideas and principles rather than historical information: the victory over Sisera is achieved in a holy war conducted under the leadership of Yahweh.

With the final section in vv. 17-22 we move into a different atmosphere, one in which, as is often the case in old traditional materials, there are three characters, but only two in action at any one time. In the event involving these three history is made; circumstantial detail is provided, and the whole account is colourful and lively in a manner comparable to the story of Ehud in Judg. 3. In both cases we have stories, and it is this basic tradition which, in Judg. 4, is elaborated with a historical introduction and theological commentary. The Jael tradition is, therefore, probably the oldest part of the chapter; it had a historical setting, but this is now given us only in a secondary form, confused with the Jabin story, in vv. 1-11; and it was finally developed in the context of holy war ideology which left its imprint in vv. 12-16.

The Song of Deborah in Judg. 5 has also undergone some development. It is possible to distinguish within it a victory song which celebrates the military defeat of Sisera by the tribes, and a cultic setting in which it is to Yahweh that the victory is ascribed. The song in vv. 12-30 (perhaps with vv. 6-8 as an introduction) is·a celebration of tribal victory; after the introduction, the participating and non-participating tribes are listed (vv. 13-18), the battle is vividly described (vv. 19-22), the death of Sisera at the hand of Jael is celebrated (vv. 24-27), and the song concludes with a taunt over the mother of Sisera vainly waiting for her son's victorious return (vv. 28-30). Only in the introduction and conclusion in vv. 1-11, 31, is Yahweh to the fore as leader of Israel; only here too is the typical hymnic language of the psalms to be traced (Pss. 18.7ff.; 50.2ff.; 77.16ff.). The setting into which the introduction and conclusion have brought the Song of Deborah is that of the cultic praise of Yahweh; it is now a psalm used in temple worship.

This approach seems to be the most satisfactory and appropriate way of accounting for the different emphases within the poem, and of explaining the lack of formal consistency which is reflected in the various titles which have been given to it: it has been called a victory ode, a psalm of thanksgiving, a liturgical composition. Such titles find some justification in the Song but none is wholly appropriate. The Song does not have the unity which they presuppose, and each title reflects something of the nature of the Song at different stages of its development. Basically it is a victory song which praises the bravery of the warriors of Israel and their commanders; their war was fought for political reasons (vv. 6-8), and their victory was secured by the heroic deed of Jael. This was not a war of Yahweh; it was by the stars of heaven and the torrent Kishon that the tribes were supported. It is only at a later stage that this victory song has become a commemoration of Yahweh's 'triumphs' (v. 11) and a celebration of those who offered themselves as the people of Yahweh against the enemies of Yahweh (vv. 11, 31). Through this reinterpretation the event is incorporated into the saving history, and becomes a victory of Yahweh over his and Israel's foes.

The basic victory song is one of the oldest poetic compositions in the Old Testament. It has points of contact with the prose tradition in Judg. 4, especially in the prominent role assigned to Jael, but it has differences also: here the listing of participants in the battle, and the battle description itself, do not represent later historicizing and theologizing elements. The song undoubtedly originated independently of the prose tradition, but its history was not without contact with that prose tradition. Judg. 5.18, a tribal saying similar to those of Gen. 49 and Deut. 33, is probably an addition which in its reference to the 'heights ($m^e r\hat{o}m\hat{e}$) of the field', reflects the influence of the Jabin tradition, according to which (Josh. 11.5, 7) the victory took place at Merom. Both the prose and the poetry seem, therefore, to

show influence from that same Jabin tradition. This would in turn
indicate that, from a relatively early stage of their development, none
of the three was transmitted without contact with the others.

It is at any rate clear that the prose tradition of Judg. 4 and the
poem of Judg. 5 were together part of the basic collection of deliverer
stories before the framework was added. The first three elements of
that framework appear in Judg. 4.1-2, the fifth element in 4.23 and
the last in 5.31. As with the Ehud tradition, so also here it is at the
conclusion of a long history of development that the framework has
set the event in the context of the sin of Israel and Yahweh's response
to Israel's cry for deliverance.

Judg. 6–9, the story of Gideon's deliverance of Israel from Midian,
with the appendix on Abimelech, is the result of a complex literary
history which has brought together into a very uneasy relationship a
wide variety of clearly quite independent materials. Some of these
represent traditions of varying age and origin, others are compositions
intended to unite those traditions. After the introduction in Judg. 6.1-
10, the call of Gideon is related in 6.11-17 followed by two altar
stories in 6.18-24 and 6.25-32. An additional historical introduction
in Judg. 6.33-35 is succeeded by Gideon's testing of the divine
promise of deliverance (6.36-40), and the story of his victory over
Midian (7.1–8.3). A further pursuit of the Midianites (8.4-21)
culminates in the offer to Gideon of kingship (8.22-23), and his
making of a golden ephod (8.24-27). Following the conclusion to the
Midian story (8.28), Gideon's connection with Shechem is established
(8.29-32), as an introduction to the story of how his son Abimelech
had himself made king there and eventually met his death (8.33–
9.57).

If the chapters are indeed composite, as this outline would itself
suggest, then the possibility exists that one feature which serves as a
link holding together some of the major elements, namely the
identification of Gideon and Jerubbaal as one and the same individual,
is a fiction. Parallels to the situation of the same individual bearing
two different names certainly exist (for example, Azariah and Uzziah
in 2 Kings 14.21; 15.13), but in the present instance there are strong
indications that the identification is secondary. Gideon is the name
used in chs. 6–8, with the exception of 6.32; 7.1; 8.29, 35, where
Jerubbaal also appears, while Jerubbaal alone is the name used in ch.
9. It is in the context of the story of Abimelech's kingship in Shechem
that the name Jerubbaal is really rooted, while that of Gideon is

connected with the defeat of the Midianites. Why the two should have been identified is, of course, the major problem with any theory that they were originally independent figures; but in the light of what we have already seen in connection with the influence of the Jabin tradition in Judg. 4.1-11, one cannot assign overriding importance to that objection. It may be simply because both Gideon and Jerubbaal came from Ophrah or came to be associated with Ophrah, that the traditions connected with both were in the course of time related.

The Gideon tradition in Judg. 6–8 is in itself complex. After the general introduction the story proper begins with the literary form of the call narrative (6.11-17). Following a prophetic pattern which is otherwise attested also for the call of Moses in Ex. 3, so the call of Gideon takes place as the answer of God to the lament of the oppressed people (Ex. 3.9f.; Judg. 6.13). Having been commissioned, both Moses and Gideon object (Ex. 3.11; Judg. 6.15); both are assured of the presence of Yahweh (Ex. 3.12; Judg. 6.16); and both seek a sign (Ex. 3.12; Judg. 6.17). This call story is now secondarily connected to the cult legend of the sanctuary of Ophrah (6.18-24), which relates how and why that sanctuary was founded. Judg. 6.25-32 is an independent tradition telling not of the foundation of a sanctuary but of the change of a sanctuary of Baal to one of Yahweh. It has been secondarily used to explain the application of the name Jerubbaal to Gideon (v. 32), a use which presupposes that this identification had, for other reasons, already been made. The tradition of Gideon's defeat of the Midianites (6.33–8.3) probably originally related it as a victory achieved by Gideon with three hundred men of his clan of the Abiezrites. In the course of its adoption as a tradition of Israel, the involvement with Gideon also of Zebulon, Naphtali, Asher, Manasseh and Ephraim, the tribes which would be affected by a Midianite incursion into Jezreel (6.33), has been made explicit (6.35; 7.23f.). Further supplementation has brought in the story of Gideon's pursuit and massacre of Zebah and Zalmunna, identified as Midianite kings (8.4-21). The remaining elements of the Gideon tradition— his refusal of kingship, making an ephod, his descendants and connection with Shechem— are in varying ways related to the identification of Gideon with Jerubbaal the father of Abimelech, and they served at a very developed stage of the tradition to introduce the conditions within which an attempt was made by Abimelech to establish kingship in Israel.

The Abimelech story also shows only a superficial uniformity. The story of Gaal and his attempt to mount a revolt against the kingship of Abimelech in Shechem is a basic and independent element in 9.26-41; it is now framed by an account of Abimelech's kingship, his destruction of Shechem and siege of Thebez in the course of which he met his death. Into that account the parable of Jotham and the confirmation of the threat it contained have been inserted in vv. 7-21, 46-49. The oldest part of the Abimelech tradition is the story of Gaal's attempted revolt. That story has been greatly modified by the new context into which it was brought; this described Abimelech's being made king (vv. 1-6), his dispute with Shechem (vv. 22-25, 42-45) and his death at Thebez (vv. 50-54, 56). This account has taken up elements of the Gaal tradition: Shechem is not the residence of Abimelech; there is a temple in the city and a tree sanctuary; the army is divided into companies for battle and the decisive battle takes place at the city gate. The intention, however, was to transform that older story: it was originally concerned to show the futility of rebellion against the king; it has been transformed into a story directed against a monarchy founded on murder. The addition of the Jotham fable and its consequences extended the reference of the Abimelech story: a monarchy founded on murder does not just itself come to ruin, but it pulls down with it all those who were in any way implicated in its inauguration.

The contexts within which the Gideon–Abimelech tradition were developed are difficult to fix; however, the prophetic form used to express the call of Gideon, and the story of the overthrow of the altar of Baal, are both probably to be related to the activities of prophetic circles especially in the later northern kingdom. The later years of the history of that kingdom, when dynasties were overthrown with regular inevitability, must also form the background for the development of the Abimelech tradition into a story directed against monarchy founded on murder. Whatever the detail may be at this point, it is the developed Gideon–Abimelech tradition which lay before the one who inserted the framework: the first two elements appear in 6.1, the third in 6.6 and the last two in 8.28. The Abimelech story, by its very nature, had to stand outside that framework; but it reinforced the statement of the framework insofar as it provided concrete illustration of the way in which salvation was not to be achieved, by relying on the leadership of a human king.

This first collection of stories comprising traditions on Ehud, Deborah–Barak and Gideon–Abimelech has a long history which goes back to the rise and gradual elaboration of individual traditions. The collection, made before the introduction of the framework, ✗ presented the traditions as stories of holy wars of Israel under the leadership of Yahweh. It is a collection which was made probably in prophetic circles of the northern kingdom: it is to the territory of the northern kingdom that the traditions belong, and it is in prophecy rather than kingship that divinely inspired leadership of Israel was to be found. While the old collection promoted charismatic leadership over monarchy founded on violence, the framework introduced a more thoroughly didactic note. Divinely inspired leadership was required because of the sin of (northern) Israel, and the monarchy which was established there was illegitimate. This presentation could only tend to justify the Judean kingdom, especially perhaps after the destruction suffered by the north. So the framework may have been added to the old collection in Judah after the fall of the northern ✗ kingdom to Assyria.

## ii. *Othniel in Judg. 3.7-11*

The story of Othniel has all the elements of the framework and yet it is distinct from the other stories in some respects. There is almost no old tradition here; apart from the proper names 'Othniel the son of Kenaz, Caleb's younger brother' and 'Cushan-rishathaim king of Mesopotamia', the material is practically all formulaic. As far as the latter is concerned, we find not only the familiar framework formulae, but additional similar expressions: 'forgetting the Lord their God, and serving the Baals and the Asheroth' (v. 7), 'the anger of the Lord was kindled against Israel' (v. 8), 'the Spirit of the Lord came upon him, and he judged Israel' (v. 10). These additional elements function to elaborate the usual framework formulae and to draw out implications which are not otherwise made explicit by the framework.

The Othniel story would thus appear to be dependent on and a development of the framework; it has been set here as an introduction, giving a typical example of events in the period. It is a model of what is to come. Furthermore, insofar as it involves the Judean clan of Caleb it brings Judah, hitherto unnoticed in the deliverer stories, into the history of the period. That may indicate a Judean background for the editor responsible for placing the Othniel story here; and since the Othniel story, though probably from a hand later than that responsible for the framework to the other deliverer stories, is nevertheless closely related to this framework, the story may add further support to the possibility already mentioned that the work of adding the framework was carried out in Judean circles.

### iii. *Jephthah and Samson in Judg. 10.6–12.6; 13–16*

The Jephthah story has often been included as one of the basic constituents of the first collection of deliverer stories. However, it is a striking fact that the links which make the connection belong almost exclusively to an extended introduction to the Jephthah story in Judg. 10.6-16. Outside that introduction there is only the statement 'So the Ammonites were subdued before the people of Israel' (Judg. 11.33), the fifth element of the framework. The introduction in Judg. 10.6-16 includes, however, not only the first three elements of the framework (vv. 6, 7, 10), but very much else besides. The additional material includes general and formulaic expressions describing the anger of Yahweh, Israel's oppression by Philistines and Ammonites, Israel's acknowledgment of sin and repentance. Moreover, as a whole it gives expression to a theology much more explicitly developed than anything found in earlier framework passages. Israel's sin lay in serving the Baals, the Ashtaroth and the foreign gods; their cry to Yahweh is not only a cry from oppression but leads directly into an acknowledgment of sin, and it is to this that Yahweh responds in indignation. The framework of the deliverer stories is here extended beyond the form it had with Othniel, and we shall see shortly that the introduction to Jephthah is in fact from a hand later than that responsible for Judg. 3.7-11. This must imply that the Jephthah story was brought into its present context as a later supplement to the already existing collection of deliverer stories, introduced by the Othniel story. Moreover, it is not only the older framework as such, but the developed form of that framework with the Othniel tradition, which has influenced the Jephthah tradition elsewhere. So, as with Othniel (Judg. 3.10), it is related also of Jephthah that 'the Spirit of the Lord came upon Jephthah' (Judg. 11.29), and 'the Lord gave them into his hand' (v. 32).

This does not mean, of course, that the Jephthah tradition is itself late. In fact, like the other deliverer stories, it shows every sign of having developed over a long period of time. The various sections into which the story falls are of uncertain relationship to each other in terms of their relative chronology, but their original independence is unmistakable. The basic story of Jephthah's becoming leader in Gilead and his defeat of the Ammonites is contained in Judg. 11.1-11,

29-33. To this story there are now attached: a long interpolation in Judg. 11.12-28, concerned apparently with relations between Israel and Moab rather than Ammon, and intended to uphold Israel's right to territory in east Jordan between the Arnon and the Jabbok; a cult legend in Judg. 11.34-40 explaining an otherwise unattested rite (Jer. 31.15 indicates a parallel custom) of ceremonial mourning by the women of Israel; and finally a composite account of legendary character dealing with relations between Gilead and Ephraim (Judg. 12.1-6). It is likely that all of these had already been brought together to form the Jephthah story before it was provided with its extended introduction in Judg. 10.6-16 attaching it to the existing collection of stories of deliverers.

Judg. 10.6-16 refers to oppression by not only the Ammonites but also the Philistines. This passage was intended, therefore, to introduce both Jephthah and Samson, for it is Philistine oppression which forms the background to chs. 13–16. The Samson story must then also be a late accretion to the book of deliverers; this is confirmed by the fact that the framework elements here are minimal, only the first two appearing in Judg. 13.1. The conclusions to the Samson saga in Judg. 15.20 and 16.31 use formulae which appear otherwise in connection with the minor judges in Judg. 10.1-5 and 12.7-15. This would indicate that with the extension of the collection of deliverer stories to include the accounts of Jephthah and Samson we are in a time which saw also the inclusion of that list of minor judges.

The Samson stories are of a type rather different from those of the deliverers. The two cycles in chs. 14–15 and ch. 16, to which the birth story of ch. 13 is a later introduction, describe no deliverance wrought by Yahweh through Samson; they are folk tales in which Samson's adventures with a woman who betrays him to the Philistines form the common theme. The distinctive features of the Samson saga are striking: though Yahweh is at work here in answering Samson's prayer (Judg. 15.18f.; 16.28ff.), it is Samson himself who is the hero; not, however, in the sense of one who saves his compatriots, but in the sense of the hero of popular fantasy: 'first in success with the female sex, first in bodily strength, courage and fondness for brawling, and first in mother-wit' (Budde, quoted in Burney).

Samson, though a hero of the tribe of Dan, also has a link with Judah (Judg. 15.9ff.); this could be taken as further indication of the independence of this figure from the old collection of Israelite deliverers and as a further link with the later stage of editing and

expanding that collecton which we have seen to have a possible
Judean background.

## iv. *The minor judges in Judg. 10.1-5; 12.7-15*

Earlier in this chapter we defined the basic characteristic of the
central section of the book of Judges as the combination of stories of
deliverers with the list of minor judges, Jephthah, who occurs in both
contexts, forming the link between them. It is now clear that the
matter is considerably more complex than that, especially because
the story of Jephthah, being itself a secondary addition to the
collection of deliverer stories, cannot be seen as the simple key to the
combination of deliverers and minor judges. In fact, there is considerable probability that the addition of the Jephthah story to the
collection of deliverer stories took place not before but along with the
combination of deliverers with the minor judges. The work of the
editor responsible for this connection was, therefore, much more
extensive and creative and much less simply mechanical than would
otherwise appear: the connection was made not simply on the basis
of the appearance of Jephthah among both deliverers and minor
judges, but in the context of a more elaborate expansion of the
collection of deliverer stories to include the Jephthah and Samson
stories along with the list of minor judges. That the list of minor
judges was introduced along with the Jephthah and Samson stories is
indicated not just by the fact that the Jephthah story is framed by the
two parts into which the list of minor judges has been divided, but
also by the fact that it is from the list of minor judges, the presence of
which is therefore presupposed, that the formula 'he judged Israel',
used of Samson in Judg. 15.20 and 16.31, has been taken.

It is, therefore, to a late stage in the development of the book of
Judges that the introduction of the list of minor judges belongs. As
with the Jephthah and Samson stories this does not, of course, carry
any necessary implication with respect to the age of that list of minor
judges. In fact, the list has always impressed scholars as an original
and authentic document from the period of the judges. It has a
common pattern in which each judge is connected with his predecessor
by the words 'after him', of each it is said that 'he judged Israel
for . . . years', and of each it is recorded that '(he) died and was buried
in . . . ' The use of the verbs 'arose' and 'deliver' in Judg. 10.1 and
'arose' in Judg. 10.3 is probably the result of secondary assimilation
to the language of the deliverer stories, after the combination of the

two literary forms was made; the verb 'judged', which appears in Judg. 12.8, 11, 13, was probably the original verb, and so a further constant element of this list of minor judges. The question of its background is one to which we shall return in a later chapter; for the moment it is sufficient to emphasize that the list probably represents an old source, even though it was only at a relatively advanced stage in the development of the central part of the book of Judges that the combination between it and the collection of deliverer stories was effected.

### v. *The introduction in Judg. 2.11–3.6*

The combination of the old collection of deliverer stories (including its model introduction in Judg. 3.7-11) with the Jephthah and Samson stories and with the list of minor judges represented a major step in the editorial development of what became the central section of the book of Judges. The intention of the editor responsible for it could not have been fulfilled simply by the provision here and there of editorial notes and linking phrases. Rather, it was necessary to provide a new introduction to this compilation, and it is this which is to be found now in Judg. 2.11–3.6. This is not a uniform passage, and we must discuss at least in general terms its development, for it is here that we meet in the first instance the editor's own introduction to his compilation of the sources we have already discerned, and, secondly, a revision of that introduction which constitutes the last editorial stage in the development of this central section of the book.

In Judg. 2.11-13 Israel's apostasy is described in different terms: on the one hand they worship the Baals, that is the gods of the land of Canaan; on the other they worship the gods of the peoples around them. Given the fact that the verses are certainly overfull, it is the latter presentation which is most probably the later of the two, for the peoples around Israel, as we read further in vv. 14f., function not as a cause of Israel's apostasy but rather as the means by which Yahweh punishes Israel for sin. Judg. 2.17 is likewise a later addition: it has caused a repetition of part of v. 16 in v. 18 and, moreover, it is incompatible with v. 19 insofar as the latter clearly implies that Israel did listen to the judges raised up by Yahweh. Judg. 2.19 comes to its own conclusion, and v. 20 introduces a quite new section with a new theme. This new subject is that of Israel in conflict with the peoples of the land which they have not been able fully to occupy; the conquest has been incomplete, and the peoples who remain are left in the land in order to test Israel's faithfulness to Yahweh.

Thus, there is here a basic narrative (Judg. 2.11, 12a, 13b, 14-16, 18-19), which explains Israel's suffering at the hands of external enemies as Yahweh's punishment for sin; out of pity for their suffering, however, Yahweh sent judges who saved Israel from their enemies; but Israel did not learn in the end: on the death of each judge they reverted to their evil ways and did worse than before. This is the introduction to the compilation of minor judges and deliverers: they are brought together, and, despite the basic incompatibility of their functions, the judge is presented as sent by Yahweh to deliver Israel. The additions to this narrative have elaborated it and introduced a new theme: Israel served the gods of those nations into whose power Yahweh sold them and those of the land in which they dwell; this is a violation of Yahweh's covenant commandments, and for this Yahweh will not aid Israel in the completion of their conquest and occupation of the land.

The introduction to the Jephthah story in Judg. 10.6-16 is remarkably similar in thought and structure: here too a basic text (vv. 6a, 7-9) describes Israel's sin in serving the Baals and Ashtaroth, and its punishment through being sold into the power of enemies outside the land; this expresses the theme of the basic text of Judg. 2.11ff., and must be part of that same editor's work in bringing together his varied sources into one compilation. The basic text here too has been edited to introduce, in v. 6b, the gods of the peoples outside the land; and vv. 10-16 presuppose the later editor's work in Judg. 2.20ff., in that they affirm that the breach of covenant there described may be forgiven and restoration will become possible when Israel repents and returns to Yahweh. Thus, Judg. 2.11ff. and 10.6ff. both contain basic texts from the same hand, which have been later supplemented, again by one hand, this being the final stage of editorial work in the central part of the book. It is to this latest stage of editing the central section of Judges that the introduction of covenant categories belongs: Israel's sin, as a result of which it was sold into the power of its enemies, consisted in the service of other gods and breach of the covenant commandments of Yahweh.

## D. The History of Origin of the Book of Judges

We can briefly review our findings on the development of the book of Judges as follows. The basic material consists primarily of stories of Ehud, Deborah–Barak and Gideon–Abimelech. These were brought together as accounts of Yahweh's deliverance of Israel in holy war. This collection was given a new theological presentation through the addition of a distinctive framework which set the events described in a sin–punishment–deliverance context. The collection of deliverer stories then received a supplement in the form of the Othniel story of Judg. 3.7-11. The next stage of the literary history is the major step in the formation of the book: it involved the addition to the existing collection of a number of hitherto independent stories, the stories of Jephthah and Samson, and the list of minor judges. At the same time introductory passages were composed in Judg. 2.11ff. and 10.6ff., in order to stengthen the unity of the new compilation: the minor judges and deliverers (the latter now including Jephthah and Samson) succeeded one another as judges sent by Yahweh to deliver Israel from distress. Thus the heart of the book was created. What happened afterwards was a modification of this: the introductions in Judg. 2.11ff. and 10.6ff. were edited in order to introduce the notion of a covenant relationship which was violated by Israel's sin and which accounted for their inability fully to occupy the land.

So the central section of Judges was completed and therewith the major part of that section of the whole deuteronomistic history which related to the period between the conquest and the rise of the monarchy. The book of Judges as we now have it came about when, finally, the prologue and epilogue in Judg. 1.1–2.5 and chs. 17–21 were added, thus separating off the tradition of the judges from all that preceded and followed. These last additions are clear interruptions to the flow of the deuteronomistic history and cannot be assigned very easily to the work of deuteronomistic editors. The main contribution of the deuteronomistic school to the book of Judges lies, first, in that major step in the development of the central section in which the collection of deliverer stories, the list of minor judges and the stories of Jephthah and Samson were all brought together with introductions in Judg. 2.11ff. and 10.6ff.; and, secondly, in a much less extensive way, in the editing of these introductions to bring in a new emphasis on the commandments of Yahweh and his covenant relationship with Israel. In these two steps, deuteronomistic editing of the book of Judges is in line with the work of that school throughout the deuteronomistic history. The cyclical presentation of history, which has been emphasized as typical of the book of Judges, is part of its pre-deuteronomistic development, while the deuteronomistic editing in fact modified that presentation by describing the history in linear terms as a time of increasing sin (Judg. 2.19); the covenant categories which appear in the later deuteronomistic editing of Judges are likewise the concerns of late deuteronomistic editing through the deuteronomistic history.

## For Further Reading

### I

Commentaries on Judges:

R.G. Boling, *Judges* (Anchor Bible; New York: Doubleday, 1975).
C.F. Burney, *The Book of Judges* (London: Rivingtons, 1930).
J. Gray, *Joshua, Judges, Ruth* (New Century Bible; London: Nelson, 1967).
G.F. Moore, *Judges* (International Critical Commentary; Edinburgh: T. and T. Clark, 1895).
J.A. Soggin, *Judges* (Old Testament Library; London: SCM, and Philadelphia: Westminster, 1981).

### II

On the deuteronomistic history:

M. Noth, *Überlieferungsgeschichtliche Studien* (Tübingen: Max Niemeyer Verlag, 1943; 2nd edn, 1957), 1-110 (= *The Deuteronomistic History* [JSOT Supplement Series, 15; Sheffield: JSOT, 1981]); G. Fohrer, *Introduction to the Old Testament* (Nashville: Abingdon Press, 1968, and London: SPCK, 1970), 192-95; F.M. Cross, 'The Structure of the Deuteronomic History', *Canaanite Myth and Hebrew Epic* (Cambridge, Mass.: Harvard University Press, 1973), 274-89; A.D.H. Mayes, *The Story of Israel between Settlement and Exile: a Redactional Study of the Deuteronomistic History* (London: SCM, 1983).

### III

General works on Judges:

E. Täubler, *Biblische Studien: Die Epoche der Richter* (Tübingen:

J.C.B. Mohr, 1958); W. Richter, *Die Bearbeitungen des 'Retterbuches' in der deuteronomischen Epoche* (BBB, 21; Bonn: Peter Hanstein Verlag, 1964); W. Richter, *Traditionsgeschichtliche Untersuchungen zum Richterbuch* (BBB, 18; Bonn: Peter Hanstein Verlag, 2nd edn, 1966); a full German summary of Richter's work in I. Schlauri, 'W. Richters Beitrag zur Redaktionsgeschichte des Richterbuches', *Bib* 54 (1973), 367-403; shorter English summaries in D.A. Knight, *Rediscovering the Traditions of Israel* (SBL Dissertation Series, 9; rev. edn, Missoula: Scholars Press, 1975), 182-86; and A.D.H. Mayes, *The Story of Israel between Settlement and Exile* (London: SCM, 1983), 58-80.

## IV

Special Studies:

(a) On the monarchic background of Judg. 1.1–2.5; 17–21
B. Halpern, *The Emergence of Israel in Canaan* (Chico: Scholars Press, 1983), 179-83; F. Crüsemann, *Der Widerstand gegen das Königtum* (WMANT, 49; Neukirchen-Vluyn: Neukirchener Verlag, 1978), 155-67.

(b) On the Ehud story
R. Alter, *The Art of Biblical Narrative* (New York: Basic Books, Inc., and London: George Allen and Unwin, 1981), 37-41.

(c) On the Deborah–Barak story
A.D.H. Mayes, *Israel in the Period of the Judges* (London: SCM, and Naperville: A.R. Allenson, 1974), 84-92; A. Globe, 'The Literary Structure and History of the Song of Deborah', *JBL* 93 (1974), 493-512; M.D. Coogan, 'A Structural and Literary Analysis of the Song of Deborah', *CBQ* 40 (1978), 146-66; D.F. Murray, 'Narrative Structure and Technique in the Deborah–Barak Story (Judges IV 4-22)', VTS 30 (1979), 155-89; H.P. Müller, 'Der Aufbau des Deboraliedes', *VT* 16 (1966), 446-59.

(d) On the Gideon–Abimelech story
W. Beyerlin, 'Geschichte und heilsgeschichtliche Traditionsbildung im Alten Testament. Ein Beitrag zur Traditionsgeschichte von Richter VI–VIII', *VT* 13 (1963), 1-25; B. Lindars, 'Gideon and Kingship', *JTS* 16 (1965), 315-26; J.A. Emerton, 'Gideon and Jerubbaal', *JTS* 27 (1976), 289-312; V. Fritz, 'Abimelech und Sichem

in Jdc IX', *VT* 32 (1982), 129-44; B. Lindars, 'Jotham's Fable: a new form critical analysis', *JTS* 24 (1973), 355-66.

(e) On the Jephthah story
W. Richter, 'Die Überlieferungen um Jephtah, Ri 10,17–12,6', *Bib* 47 (1966), 485-556; J.A. Soggin, *Judges* (Old Testament Library; London: SCM, and Philadelphia: Westminster Press, 1981), 201-22.

(f) On the Samson story
J. Blenkinsopp, 'Structure and Style in Judges 13–16', *JBL* 82 (1963), 65-76; U. Simon, 'Samson and the Heroic', *Ways of Reading the Bible* (edited by M. Wadsworth; Brighton: Harvester Press, 1981), 154-67; J. Cheryl Exum, 'Aspects of Symmetry and Balance in the Samson Saga', *JSOT* 19 (1981), 3-29; Exum, 'The Theological Dimension of the Samson Saga', *VT* 33 (1983), 30-45.

# 2

## THE SOCIAL CONTEXT OF EVENTS RELATED IN JUDGES

### A. Israel in the Ancient Near East

THE OLDEST material in the book of Judges may certainly be traced back to actual events and people of the pre-monarchic period. However, our study in the previous chapter of these oldest traditions did not lead us to a clear picture of Israel as such in the period of the judges. The events on which the traditions rest were isolated and of limited significance, as indeed were also the charismatic deliverers and judges. It is difficult from such fragments to derive anything like a sense of the life and history of a people Israel.

We shall see in the next chapter that one of the fundamental requirements of a satisfactory historical reconstruction, the determination of a chronological framework, is also largely lost to us for the period of the judges. This increases the isolation of those events and personalities which belong to the period, and makes even more remote the possibility of anything like an adequate historical understanding. However, even if the chance of establishing a history of pre-monarchic Israel, in terms of a chronological sequence of events, is slight, it is still possible to create a context of understanding for these events in a different sense. The events of the period of the judges, whatever the precise form they may have taken and whatever their precise chronological relationship, were largely determined by the social and cultural forces at work in the people involved in that history. The essential nature of the history is, therefore, to be discovered not simply from reliable chronology, but much more rather from a good understanding of the nature of the society which experienced that history. The study of the nature of Israelite society is not a dispensable preliminary to the reconstruction of the history; rather the society and its history run together, so that only on the basis of an understanding of both will it be possible to speak of Israel in the period of the judges. Thus, our reconstruction may indeed be defective because important historical information is unattainable; but the nature of the history may still in general terms at least be reliably presented through rescuing the events and individuals from their isolation and setting them in their proper context in Israelite society.

The nature of Israelite society will be properly appreciated only by setting it in the context of the social system which preceded and accompanied the rise of Israel. Even with the most literal reading of the biblical record such a wider setting is demanded, for it is quite clear that 'Canaanite' society was by no means simply replaced by 'Israelite' society; rather, they were closely intermingled and it was to a considerable extent in reaction to 'Canaanite' society that 'Israelite' society developed in its distinctive form. We shall begin, therefore, with a discussion of the form of Canaanite society as a context within which and against which to see the rise of Israel.

## B. Social Forms in the Environment of Israel

A variety of sources is available to allow a fairly clear reconstruction of social forms in Palestine in the time preceding and accompanying the rise of Israel. Particularly important are the Ugaritic texts, the Alalakh tablets and the Amarna letters, and these are complemented to a greater or lesser degree by other materials such as the Egyptian Execration texts and the Story of Sinuhe. There is, of course, the ever present danger of over-simplification and unjustified generalization. So, in particular, it may not readily be assumed that the form of society at Ugarit, as reflected in the texts deriving from there, is to be taken as a model which may be adopted as appropriate for the time and place with which we are here especially concerned. Ugarit, after all, lay considerably north of the Egyptian province of Canaan, and the fourteenth-century Ugaritic texts are much older than the time of pre-monarchic Israel. Moreover, apart from the geographical and temporal separation, the internal diversity inevitable within such a geographically heterogeneous country as Canaan is sufficient to discourage the application of any single model to the whole environment of Israel.

Nevertheless, the sources are by no means contradictory in the picture they present; there is, rather, diversity within a general uniformity. It is impossible to say whether all Canaanite cities of the time had a city council with certain political and adminstrative powers under the king, simply because some texts refer to such a council; yet despite uncertainty on questions such as this which are in themselves of considerable significance, there remains a functional uniformity in the system operated in the Canaanite cities which is not much disturbed by the possibility of occasional variation.

The use of the term 'urban' to characterize Canaanite society and distinguish it from the peasant-rural culture of Israel is potentially misleading. Much of the contrast which is too quickly drawn between the urban and the rural depends on an understanding of the nature of the city which is appropriate only to the age of industrialization. In the pre-industrial age the city was largely dependent (except when unusually favourably placed for trade) on the agricultural produce of its hinterland, so that a fairly thorough symbiosis of the rural and the urban was inevitable. This would be reflected in perhaps two chief respects: first, in the fact that the ruling élite in any city, which was not directly involved in agriculture but rather was devoted exclusively to government, was proportionately very small; secondly, in the fact that a large element of the population of the city would leave it daily to engage in agricultural activities, or, living in smaller rural communities, would see the city as a place of refuge from which they would never be far distanced. Thus the strong ties between the city and the country resist any easy distinction between the city and the village, the urban and the rural.

However, with reservations, that distinction may be maintained. City administration and administrators had to be supported, and this could be done only through taxation; taxes were levied on the productive sectors of society, those elements of the (lower) urban classes who, together with the rural communities, were engaged in agriculture. The social division between rulers and ruled to some extent necessarily cut across a crude distinction between urban and rural; but the information deriving from Ugarit and Alalakh, and from Syria-Palestine, fits well in general terms within the framework formed by this distinction.

### a. Ugarit and Alalakh

Both Ugarit and Alalakh, but especially the former, far surpassed the city-states of Palestine in size and wealth, and allowance must be made for this in using sources from these places to complement the material bearing directly on Palestine. None of the Palestinian cities enjoyed the potential and actual prosperity of Ugarit as a centre of trade by land and sea, and consequently none of them could compare with Ugarit in either power or development of social structure. Yet the differences are of degree rather than of fundamental principle. In every case society is characterized by distinction between a privileged ruling class and a subject population.

Thus, Ugaritic administrative texts list almost two hundred villages, of which about one hundred and thirty are said to have provided material support to the king of Ugarit in the form of taxes and obligatory services. Taxation, which was collected by royal agents, included monetary taxes together with tithes paid in grain, wine, olive oil, cattle, ploughing oxen and sheep; obligatory service included military conscription as well as forced labour in ploughing, cutting and transporting wood and working on royal building projects. Each village was responsible as a single unit for the payment of its taxes and performance of its duties, and the distribution of burdens within each village was carried through presumably on the basis of the wealth or size of family. Such a range of subject villages required a fairly complex governmental administration; and there existed in this system a means of reward and payment by which the king of Ugarit could (and did) bestow the produce of a village on certain of his high officials. This is not to say that the king was sole owner of the land, which he then bestowed on his loyal officials; he was rather the largest landowner, and royal land possession was increased both through purchase and the confiscation of the property of criminals or those who defaulted in tax payment. However, private land ownership was also known, and land could be bought, sold and inherited within the rural community. To that extent the popular use of the term 'feudal' to describe this political system is misleading. However, the characteristic social stratification and the system of land grants by which the king bound his servants in loyalty to their overlord justify our thinking at least in terms of feudal-like structures at this time.

Between the king and the free rural population on which taxes were levied there were two social layers: servants of the king, and servants of the servants of the king. To which of these any given element of the population belonged is sometimes uncertain, but it is clear that the servants of the servants of the king included the ordinary members of the many guilds of workers (for example, doorkeepers, singers, shepherds, builders, smiths, carpenters), while among the servants of the king were reckoned not only the royal officials such as the palace steward and overseer of crown property, but also the aristocratic *maryannu*. The latter was a title conferred by the king on one of his subjects, an honour which brought with it a grant of land from the royal landholdings, exemption from taxation, and perhaps also (to judge from the frequent association of the term with chariotry) membership in an élite military corps. This was a particularly privileged position which could be passed on from one generation to the next, and is perhaps the most distinctive element of the social structure represented by the city-state system.

### b. Syria-Palestine

While Ugarit displays a size and complexity, and Alalakh a precision of social stratification, which are not exactly reproduced in Syria-Palestine, the differences are more of degree than of fundamental principle. In every case society is characterized by a distinction between a privileged ruling class and a subject population on which taxation is imposed.

In the period leading up to the emergence of Israel, Canaan was a province of the Egyptian empire. Government was therefore constituted on two levels. On the upper level was the Egyptian Pharaoh who, through his adminstrators, was the ultimate authority. This authority was sometimes, especially in the fourteenth-century Amarna period, of a nominal nature; but it was maintained to a greater or lesser extent until Egypt's internal weakness and anarchy, combined with pressure from the Sea Peoples, brought its influence in Palestine to an end towards the end of the thirteenth century. On the lower level was the local authority, the rule exercised under the Pharaoh by the kings of the city-states and their governments. Each city-state had its own king and, outside occasional alliances and common submission to Egypt, was independent.

There were, as Alt has shown, considerable variations in the area of land dominated by these city-states: the more densely settled coastal plain and the plain of Esdraelon supported many city-states resulting in each one controlling a fairly limited land space, comprising the fields belonging to the city and a few villages; the mountain districts, on the other hand, were less fertile, more heavily wooded, and consequently more sparsely settled, and here the land dominated (though less effectively controlled) by any one city-state, such as Shechem under Labayu in the Amarna period, was of some considerable extent. This distinction does not, however, vitiate the uniformity of political structure by which all of these city-states were governed; what it in fact does indicate is that the system of government represented by the city-states was much more concentrated in the plains than in the mountains, and that as a result it was the population of the plains more than the population of the mountains who were more completely integrated into that form of rule. Thus, insofar as opportunities existed for the development of alternative political systems these were to be found in the mountain territories rather than in the plains.

In Palestine, therefore, the city-states had only a fairly limited extent of territory available to them, and had the additonal disadvantage of obligation to pay tribute to Egypt; thus they were inevitably considerably less prosperous than Ugarit, their lower class and peasant populations being especially impoverished. However, their social structure was fundamentally identical to that of Ugarit; this was because of the very nature of the system to which they belonged, but it was also reinforced by one factor in particular: the influence of the Hyksos in Palestine in the Amarna age. The Hyksos introduced the chariot as a means of waging war, but the material requirements associated with its maintenance strongly affected Canaanite society in general. Chariot warfare brought with it especially the rise of a professional military class which was supported as an exclusive military group by taxes levied on the subject population. This group formed a bulk of the aristocracy in the city-state, and (in this respect differing from Ugarit) constituted a significant, independent check on the power of the king. The members of the upper class formed a council which the king ignored at his peril; indeed in several city-states the king was overthrown and government was assumed by this oligarchic group. However, as in Ugarit, the burden of maintaining the ruling class, whatever the constitution of that class may have been, rested on the peasantry.

The taxation burden in Palestine was probably considerably heavier than in Ugarit for a variety of reasons: primarily, the taxed population was responsible not only for the means by which the ruling class might be supported but also for the tribute payable to the Egyptian overlord; secondly, the city-states of Syria-Palestine did not enjoy advantages accruing from trade to the same extent as Ugarit, which was a significant seaport; thirdly, the agricultural base from which taxation was derived was of limited extent, and difficult to develop or even maintain in the face of the incessant warfare which characterized relations between the city-states of Syria-Palestine. The effect of this was an extreme degree of poverty in the subject population and this, together with the strong sense of insecurity felt by the ruling class towards its subjects anyway, is reflected in site excavations in Syria-Palestine. In excavations at Tell Beit Mirsim, Taanach, Bethel and Hazor the dwellings of the rulers are seen to be of a vastly superior standard, and are often enclosed within a wall which both separated them and probably also protected them from the lower-class inhabitants (for example, potters, metal workers, textile workers) of inferior parts of the city.

The social division between ruler and ruled was, therefore, more pronounced in Syria-Palestine than at Ugarit. The taxation borne by the subject population maintained the rulers and provided the tribute for Egypt; it also supplied the needs of Egyptian expeditionary forces, protected their caravans, and supplied troops and labour for Egyptian projects. The decline of the city-states of Syria-Palestine in the Late Bronze Age, which forms the immediate background to the emergence of Israel, was in large measure due to the inability of the lower class population to sustain the impositions laid on them. Their increasing impoverishment led sometimes to their enslavement, and sometimes to flight from the ruling powers, and it encouraged the growth of disaffected alienated elements in the land, including that landless group of social outcasts known as the Habiru. The fundamental economic inability of the population to support the superstructure was exacerbated rather than ameliorated by the gradual decline of Egyptian power and influence in Canaan. This decline brought to an end the security of the trade routes through Syria-Palestine, which in turn resulted in the loss of revenue to the city-states. Palestine at the time of the emergence of Israel represented, as far as its social structure was concerned, the remnants of a city-state system which had been in a state of decline since the Amarna age.

### c. Society in the environment of Israel

We can briefly characterize the social structure of non-Israelite Canaan as follows. First, it was strictly hierarchical with a clear distinction between ruler and ruled. The king, with his nobles and professional soldiers, was supported by taxes levied on an increasingly impoverished subject population, whose alternatives to severe impositions were either slavery or rejection of the system; the latter perhaps involved (depending on the strength of the ruler to impose his will) physical flight. This was a system whose gradual decline had clear economic causes, but which nevertheless persevered until well into the Israelite period. The absorption of the city-states with their consequent loss of independence was a gradual process, and even when they eventually came under the control of David it is likely that this involved more a change of leadership than a fundamental reformation of this social system.

Secondly, the role of kinship in these societies is secondary or considerably weakened. It is true that at top and bottom, at the level of the king and at that of the rural peasant, the family was an effective element. Positions of influence and authority would be filled by the king from his family, while basic to the rural village community was the individual family. However, in the context of fiscal administration and the law it is not the family which is significant but the guild (in the city) or the village unit. The village as a whole was a single unit before the law, collectively responsible for crimes committed by its members or within its territory; it was on the village as a whole that tax was imposed and from which labour and military recruits were required. The focus here is on the locality, the land, rather than on the family which lives there.

Thirdly, while it would be simplistic both to talk in terms of 'Canaanite religion', and also to see such a religion as a pure reflection of the society in which it functioned, it seems true that the polytheism of Canaan was fitted to its social context. Religious practice was as varied as social forms, yet here too certain constants may be discerned. Religion was both polytheistic and thoroughly anthropomorphic in its mythological expression. Most prominent among the gods are El and his wife Asherah, and Baal and his sister/consort Anat. It is a mistake to over-emphasize the fertility aspects of worship among the Canaanites and to contrast this sharply with Israel's worship of Yahweh, for it is clear from the Ugaritic texts that El, with whom Yahweh had no conflict and was indeed identified, was regarded as active in nature and fertility, besides being creator god and head of the pantheon, while Baal, with the worship of whom Yahwism came into deepest conflict, gave expression to other ideas and beliefs besides that of fertility. There may have been some difference in the understanding of Baal between Canaan and Ugarit, and it is from the latter that we derive our most trustworthy picture; but Baal's remarkable lack of involvement in fertility rituals in

Ugarit is probably a much more general feature of his cult. The mythological texts relating his conflicts with Yam and Mot have to do with Baal's position as king: in his defeat of Yam he is king in the assembly of the gods, in his defeat of Mot he becomes king over the earth. As Koch has argued, these myths have nothing to do with explanations of the agricultural year, but rather give expression to ideas relating to power and authority within the context of a particular understanding of cosmic order. Baal is no nature deity, but a claimant to kingship who defeats his foes. His kingly role among the gods both reflects and sustains the monarchic system of the city-state which honours him as god.

It is right, therefore, to relate the distinctiveness of Canaanite religion to the distinctiveness of its society, and to see both of these as inseparable aspects of the culture over against which the people Israel gradually emerged. Israelite society and Israelite religion were likewise thoroughly linked, and the distinctiveness of Israelite religion over against that of Canaan cannot be treated independently of the social context within which it was nurtured. The concepts of 'nature' and 'history' are of only very limited usefulness in marking out distinctions; much more central to the religious difference between Israel and Canaan are the differences between the societies which they represented.

## C. Israelite Society in the Pre-Monarchic Period

The question of the nature of Israelite society in the pre-monarchic period cannot be covered by a discussion of the possible existence of an Israelite tribal federation. Ever since Noth gave the first thorough and systematic presentation of the theory that pre-monarchic Israel was a tribal federation with a constitution analogous to the later classical amphictyony, there has been considerable interest in the question of the nature of Israelite society as a totality. This topic is of some interest and importance, but its consideration must come not at the beginning of an attempt to understand the structure of Israelite society, but rather at its end. Whether or not such a federation existed, in social and economic terms it certainly did not lie at the basis of Israelite society, but rather could only have been created on an already existing basis, and it is this foundation which must first of all be examined. We shall be concerned here first with the basic social structure of Israel, secondly with its way of life, and thirdly with the problem of the form by which the total society may have been comprehended.

## a. Tribal society

Israel is defined by the Old Testament as a people descended from the twelve sons of Jacob, each of these sons being considered the eponymous ancestor of a tribe which is known by his name (Ex. 1.1-7). The numbers of each tribe and their constituent clans are provided (Num. 1; 26). Thus, Israel is portrayed as a 'tribal society'. A quick reading of Josh. 7.14-18 seems then to confirm that within each tribe there were several clans, and each clan comprised a number of families or households. However, this description is potentially misleading: if it implies that the people had a systematic structure in which the tribe was the basic and self-contained unit in society, within the context of which the economic and social relations of its members belonged, then our understanding of the true nature of Israel will be distorted. If this presentation is then set in the wider context of the view that tribalism represents a nomadic or semi-nomadic social structure, and that Israel's tribalism in the land is a relict of its nomadic or semi-nomadic past, then we have the ingredients for both an erroneous understanding of Israel's constitution and an unbalanced view of her history. The question of what is meant by a tribal society and by Israel's tribalism in particular has, then, some considerable importance.

A close examination of Josh. 7.14-18 shows a rather confusing picture: the command of v. 14 distinguishes clearly the first unit, the tribe, from the second unit, the clan, and both of these from the third unit, the family (English Bible translations are not consistent in their renderings for the second and third units, which are sometimes given as 'family' and 'household' respectively; here the term 'family' is used for the third unit, and the admittedly not altogether satisfactory term 'clan' for the second unit); the tribe comprises a number of clans all of which break down into families. In the description of the carrying out of the command, however, in vv. 16-18, a much less regular structure appears: 'So Joshua rose early in the morning, and he brought Israel near tribe by tribe, and the tribe of Judah was taken. And he brought near the clan of Judah and the clan of the Zerahites was taken, and he brought near the clan of the Zerahites man by man, and Zabdi was taken. And he brought near his family, man by man, and Achan, the son of Carmi, son of Zabdi, son of Zerah of the tribe of Judah was taken'.

Two points are striking here: first, unless with the LXX and some Hebrew MSS we read 'clans of Judah' for 'clan of Judah', the terms 'clan' and 'tribe' are here used of the same entity, Judah. This use of 'clan' is found also in Judg. 13.2 and 18.2 of Dan, and again of Judah in Judg. 17.7. Secondly, the command of Josh. 7.14 distinguishes the 'clan' from its constituent 'families', but in the fulfilment of the command the distinction is no longer so rigid: while Zabdi is the head of a family from which Achan is eventually taken, it is as an individual rather than as a family that Zabdi is first taken from the 'clan' of the Zerahites. Again, the use of 'clan' and 'family' almost as interchangeable terms is found elsewhere. In Gen. 24 Abraham's servant reported his master's command in the following terms: 'you shall go to my father's family and to my clan and take a wife for my son' (v. 38), and 'you shall take a wife for my son from my clan and from my father's family; then you shall be free of my oath when you come to my clan' (vv. 40f.). Here it is probably better to read the terms 'clan' and 'family' as hendiadys, that is, as an example of the use of two terms for one and the same thing, rather than as references to absolutely distinct entities. 1 Sam. 10.20f. is, unfortunately, probably a corrupt text, but if, with the RSV, we follow the LXX in restoring 'he brought near the clan of the Matrites man by man' to v. 21, then here too an individual, Saul, is drawn directly from the 'clan' rather than from the 'family'. In Josh. 2.12 (cf. also v. 18) Rahab made the spies of Israel promise to preserve her father's 'family', but in Josh. 6.23 it is the term 'clans' which is used of this group. Finally, a similar vagueness appears in 1 Sam. 9.20f.: Saul here responded to Samuel's reference to the honour which kingship will bestow on him and his family by lamenting the weakness of his clan among all the clans of his tribe; no mention is made of his 'family'.

None of this should be taken to suggest that 'tribe', 'clan' and 'family' were interchangeable terms. Clearly they were not; and the general presentation of the family, the clan and the tribe as successively wider social contexts to which the individual belonged is not an inaccurate one. However, the texts we have looked at, which are all pre-deuteronomistic, show that in reality this was no rigid social structure, and they certainly would not support the idea that tribalism meant that the 'tribe' was the significant and constant element to which smaller, less stable, social units were subordinate. There may be a certain indecisiveness in distinguishing between 'clan' and 'family', but it is a more important point that it is often (as in Gen. 24 and Josh. 2) these alone which are mentioned as the social contexts to which the individual belongs, while the 'tribe' does not appear at all. In fact it is really only in later priestly texts, especially those of Numbers (for example, Num. 1 and 26), that Israel is given a systematic constitution in terms of clearly distinguishable 'tribe', 'clan' and 'family', in which the twelve tribes form the basic framework for comprehending the totality of Israel.

In order to achieve a more secure basis for understanding Israel's social structure, one should not follow the priestly writer by looking first at the way in which the people as a whole was divided into its tribes; rather, one should seek the fundamental social unit, that to which the individual Israelite primarily belonged and within the context of which his life was ordered. From this point of view it is the 'family' and the 'clan' which assume fundamental significance. There is some suggestion, as we have noted, that the distinction between 'family' and 'clan' was not always clearly preserved, but it is clear from many references that a certain distinction did exist, and that the two can be seen to have had different though strongly related functions. Abimelech, when seeking support for his bid for kingship, spoke to 'the whole clan of his mother's family' (Judg. 9.1), that is, to all the members of the clan to which his mother's family belonged. In 2 Sam. 16.5 a certain Shimei, from the clan to which the family of Saul also belonged, opposed and cursed David. When David self-deprecatingly questioned his fitness to be son-in-law to the king Saul, he asked, 'Which is my father's clan in Israel?' (1 Sam. 18.18); this is an elliptic expression meaning 'Which is the clan to which my father's family belongs in Israel?' Both terms, 'clan' and 'family', are important for the Israelite's identity; the former is best understood to represent the larger support group within which the latter belonged.

This picture may be confirmed from two directions, first from information on the clan yielded especially by the book of Ruth, and, secondly, from legislation relating apparently to the family. The story of Ruth tells that Naomi, following the deaths of her husband Elimelech and her two sons, returned to Bethlehem with her Moabite daughter-in-law Ruth. While gleaning in the fields Ruth met Boaz, described as being 'of the clan of Elimelech' (2.1); he is also a 'relative' and a *gō'ēl* (2.20), that is, one with the duty to act as protector, whether by marrying a widow in order to ensure the continuation of the family line, or by paying off the debt of one who has been or is on the point of being enslaved for debt, or by carrying out blood revenge. Boaz, however, is not the one with primary responsibility towards Ruth in this regard, since there is a closer relative (3.12), and only after the latter has declined to function as *gō'ēl* (4.6) does Boaz take Ruth as his wife. The priestly legislation on slavery for debt in Lev. 25.48f. reflects a similar situation even if it is here formalized beyond what may actually have been the practice. The first under obligation to carry out the function of the *gō'ēl* is the brother, then the uncle, then the cousin, and finally any one belonging to the clan. The 'clan', therefore, is the group or association within which are found families; it is held together by kinship ties, and functions to maintain and if necessary restore the families which belong to it.

Yet it is clear that the family is not subordinate to the clan, but forms a real and effective unit within it. This means that the use of the term 'clan' in this context is potentially misleading. In the true clan system the clan is exogamous; that is, the clan is the basic social unit outside which marriages must be contracted; the clan rather than the family is the primary social and economic unit; property is owned by the clan rather than by the family, and work is organized within the framework of the clan rather than that of the family. The family is socially and economically subordinate, and functions primarily as the means by which the population of the clan is renewed and maintained. In Israel, however, the clan is apparently not exogamous and it is the family which is the primary social and economic unit. The endogamous nature of the Israelite clan is indicated by the patriarchal stories which allow Isaac to marry Rebekah and Jacob to marry Leah and Rachel; these are marriages of cousins on the father's side which would not be possible in a true clan system. The possibility of marriage within the Israelite clan is also indicated, though negatively, by the laws of Lev. 18.6-18: here marriage is prohibited within degrees of relationship which should be defined as family rather than clan. The unit presupposed consists of the father with his wife, together with his brothers and their wives, his sons and daughters and his sons' wives, his grandchildren with his grandsons' wives and his greatgrandchildren. This 'extended family' conforms to the unit presupposed by the affirmation of collective responsibility to the third and fourth generation in the decalogue (Ex. 20.5). It was on behalf of such a family unit that the system of redemption by the *gō'ēl* operated, and it is precisely this system which presupposes that it was within the family that property belonged. This is vividly illustrated also by the complaint brought to David by the woman of Tekoa, who related how the action of the clan threatened to extinguish completely the family line to which she belonged (2 Sam. 14.7). Thus, the family and the clan are the two significant social units in Israel. They are inter-dependent rather than independent entities, for neither exists without the other: the family is the primary unit, the clan functions as the wider association within which the families intermarry and find material aid and protection.

Compared with the family and the clan, the 'tribe' has much less form and consistency. It was both a social and a territorial entity, but was subject to strong internal modification and change. The tribe of Dan first attempted to settle west of Jerusalem, but, as a result of pressure from the Philistines or Amorites, was forced to migrate to a new settlement region far to the north (Judg. 18; cf. Judg. 1.34; Josh. 19.40-48); the reference to a Transjordanian tribe by the name of Gilead in Judg. 5.17, at a point where reference to the otherwise familiar tribe of Gad would be expected, may indicate either that Gilead was subsequently displaced by a newly immigrant tribe of Gad or that Gilead suffered internal changes leading to the rise of a new element within it named Gad. Judg. 5 also refers to a West-Jordan tribe named Machir (v. 14), at a point where one would expect reference to Manasseh; on the other hand, Num. 26.29 and 27.1 refer to Machir as the son of Manasseh and father of Gilead. This probably presupposes Machir's partial migration from West to East Jordan and its colonization there of (part of) Gilead, while those who remained in West Jordan took the name Manasseh. Similar migrations from West to East Jordan, resulting perhaps from tribal expansion which at times may have involved the formation of new tribal entities, are indicated by the settlement of East Jordan by Reuben, Gad and half Manasseh (Num. 32) and by the scornful description of the Gileadites in Judg. 12.1-6 as 'fugitives of Ephraim'. A different type of situation is to be discerned in the case of Benjamin, for there are some indications, particularly its special relationship with Ephraim (Judg. 3.15ff.; 5.14; 19-21), and the meaning of its name ('southerners'), that it originated as a split-off from the tribe of Ephraim.

Tribes could be such fluid and changeable entities because, unlike the family and the clan, they were not constituted on the basis of kinship. What did hold them together and, indeed, the forces that resulted in the first formation of such larger associations, are very difficult to discern. The living together of a number of clans would have been a factor, but not in itself sufficient; the cult functions as a unifying force, though not necessarily at a 'tribal' level; the mobilization of the popular army was essentially a matter for the clan rather than the tribe and so it can scarcely have functioned in the constitution of the tribe. However, even though there seems to have been no tribal mechanism, as opposed to clan mechanism, for issuing the call to arms, it probably was in large measure military necessity which forced along the coming together of the clans into loosely organized tribes. In addition, as the clans developed and expanded over the course of time there would soon have arisen the need to develop a means of settling, at a level above that of the clan, the inter-clan problems and disputes which would inevitably have resulted from increasingly close contact.

Gottwald has described Israel's tribalism as a deliberately formed alternative society, 'a self-constructed instrument of resistance and of decentralized self-rule', which arose in opposition to the hierarchic social system of the Canaanite city-state environment. Whether or not this is an accurate representation of the origins of this social form, it remains true that the tribal society of Israel, fundamentally based as it was on kinship and the extended family, was radically different from city-state society: social and economic influence and power were exercised from the bottom rather than from the top; social structures wider than the family and clan were loosely organized forms responding both to external pressures and to developing internal need, but they remained loose and fluid. Tribalism was an independent social and economic form, distinct from city-state society both organizationally and in its total style of life.

## b. Israel as a pastoral society

What we noted at the beginning of this chapter with regard to the relationship between urban and rural forms of life is particularly relevant at this point. The strong interdependence of the city and country, in that the city is the place of refuge and security for rural dwellers, while the country with its agriculture is the economic basis to the prosperity of the city, means that an absolute distinction between them cannot be justified; yet the distinction must be maintained at least in order to provide a framework within which

Israelite society may be understood as a rural phenomenon offering a social structure quite different from the hierarchical system of the Canaanite city-states. The degree of relationship between the urban and the rural was variable: at one point they were closely inter-dependent, at another they were practically independent. Villages situated in close proximity to the city-states were socially and economically closely bound in with those city-states; rural commun-ities established outside the sphere of influence of the city-states maintained and developed their own structures. Tribal Israel was established sometimes (as in the case of Issachar) close to the city-state culture of the plains, but mainly in the less accessible mountain regions which remained outside city-state control and where the forms of government and society characteristic of the city-states exercised little influence.

Cities do occasionally feature in the traditions of Israel in the period of the judges, both in the tradition of the deliverers and in that of the 'minor judges': so, for example, it is from the city of Kedesh in Naphtali that Barak came at Deborah's call (Judg. 4.6), the cities of Ophrah, Succoth and Penuel feature in the Gideon tradition (Judg. 6.11, 24; 8.5-9), while the minor judge Tola lived at Shamir, and Jair had thirty cities in Gilead (Judg. 10.1,4). However, these are certainly not references to independent city-states with a hierarchic social structure, but rather to more or less developed settlements integrated into a rural tribal social system. The status of Succoth and Penuel as Israelite cities is perhaps open to doubt, since they exhibit consider-able independence over against Gideon; moreover, their rulers, and those of the tribe of Issachar, are known as 'princes' (*śārîm*, Judg. 5.15; 8.6). However, as Thiel notes, although there can be no question but that the cognate Akkadian term *šarru* belongs originally to the culture of the developed state, the term is also frequently used for tribal leaders in the Mari texts. The 'cities' of Israel in the pre-monarchic period were in general undoubtedly very much part of a rural tribal society rather than of an urban civilization. Even for some considerable time after the rise of the monarchy and the adoption at the same time of many of the characteristics of the city-state culture, such as the professional army and the tax structure required to support it and the royal court, it is likely that, outside the capital and other centres especially on the periphery or in less secure parts of the kingdom, the city in Israel remained more or less fully integrated into rural life; sometimes it was little more than an enlarged rural type settlement, distinct from a village only in having a defensive wall.

It is consistent with this distinctiveness of tribal society from city-state culture that tribal society is not characterized by a thorough-going division of labour and even less by the guilds of workers which feature in the city-state context. The information available here is far from plentiful, but what there is shows tribal society as a pastoral-agricultural form of life with none of the specialisms already mentioned as typical of the city-state culture. The Gideon story describes the Midianite oppression as taking the form of raids on Israelite fields to destroy and loot crops and animals (Judg. 6.1-6); and it may indeed be assumed that the growing of wheat and barley, the tending of sheep, goats and cattle and the cultivation of vineyards, were in one form or another generally characteristic of life in Israelite tribal society. It was while ploughing that Saul first heard of the plight of Jabesh-gilead (1 Sam. 11), while it was apparently mainly animal husbandry that Nabal practised (1 Sam. 25:2). It is unlikely that outside this agricultural-pastoral mix there was any significant contribution to the tribal economy; and even within it, it is perhaps at this stage too early for such specialisms to have appeared as, for example, the later wine industry at Gibeon.

We may confirm and fill out this picture by reference to the patriarchal traditions. These are directly relevant to the context of pre-monarchic Israel, for the present ordering of Pentateuchal materials according to which the patriarchs were early ancestors of the later Israel is certainly secondary. In the patriarchs we have nuclear Israel, families living a form of life in Palestine that was typically Israelite-tribal, especially before the foundation of the Israelite state. Here too it is a mixture of agriculture and animal husbandry which forms the economic basis of life. All three patriarchs are said to have had sheep and cattle (Gen. 12.16; 20.14; 21.27; 26.14; 32.5), Abraham had meal which Sarah used in order to prepare cakes for his visitors (Gen. 18.6), Isaac 'sowed in that land, and reaped in the same year a hundredfold' (Gen. 26.12), and his blessing of Jacob included the prayer for 'plenty of grain and wine' (27.28). Tribal society thus involved a strong attachment to agriculture and the tending of sheep and cattle.

It has been widely thought that the non-specialized and kinship-based form of life which Israelite tribalism represents was a survival from a nomadic or semi-nomadic past, that this society was peculiarly appropriate to and developed out of the exigencies of wilderness existence, and that with settlement it gradually broke down so that the original significance of tribalism, involving the fierce loyalty of the individual to his tribe, came to be replaced eventually by a system in which the individual and his now weakened clan came to be subordinated to the centralized state. According to this understanding, the crucial event, which marked the watershed between tribe and state, was settlement in the land, the semi-nomad having until then led a form of life sharply contrasted with the life of the settled farmer.

It is now apparent, however, both from anthropological theory in general and from a more balanced appreciation of the Old Testament texts themselves, that this understanding is inaccurate. There was no general evolutionary development from hunter to nomad or semi-nomad and from there to a settled, agricultural form of life, which is the scheme presupposed by the theory that nomadism or semi-nomadism was the life style of the Israelite tribes before they settled in the land. Certainly, men hunted and gathered food before they grew it, but it is only in this sense that nomadism can be said to be a pre-settlement form of existence. The semi-nomadic herding of small cattle and sheep, on the other hand, does not represent an independent form of life preceding settlement; rather semi-nomadism belongs with agriculture and the settled life as a single economic mode of existence. Semi-nomadism involved the breeding of livestock and regular seasonal migration, or transhumance, in search of pasture; it has been described as a specialized offshoot of the settled, agricultural way of life, practised perhaps only for part of the year by a segment of a larger social group which was otherwise fully settled. Thus, the dichotomy in society existed not between the nomadic or semi-nomadic on the one hand and the settled on the other, but between the urban and the rural way of life, and the latter included both agriculture and, to a limited extent, pastoral nomadism. The popular understanding of the nomad as a proud desert dweller, independent of and contemptuous towards the life of the settled farmer, is based on modern conditions and has no pertinence to the ancient Near East and particularly to Israel.

This has relevance obviously to the question of Israel's origins and settlement of the land, rather than to Israel in the period of the judges, for Israelite origins have been widely discussed within the context of an erroneous understanding of semi-nomadism. The reconstruction of Alt, which set Israel's settlement in the overall context of semi-nomadic transhumance, presupposed the idea that the social dichotomy existed between settled and semi-nomad, that semi-nomads were wanderers on the fringe between the desert and fruitful land, pressing in on and hungry for the fertile territory largely controlled by the Canaanites, and succeeding eventually in infiltrating parts of the fertile land which were least under Canaanite domination. This reconstruction, however, must now be modified to take account of the fact that semi-nomadism belongs with agriculture, and that its followers are indigenous inhabitants of the land along with the farmer. Israel's patriarchal origins lie within the rural tribal socio-economic sector within Palestine, and its tribal constitution demands no presuppostion of an origin outside the borders of the land. The mixture of agriculture and sheep-breeding which characterizes the life of tribal Israel is found also with the so-called semi-nomads of the Mari texts, who have frequently been brought forward as an analogy to support the thesis of Israel's semi-nomadic origins. Tribalism is not only compatible with settlement, but in fact belongs to that non-urban mode of life which, including both agriculture and stock-breeding, is an essential constituent of existence in the fertile land.

The whole question has, however, some relevance also to the nature of pre-monarchic Israel, for it is precisely the view that tribalism is a survival from a nomadic or semi-nomadic past which has encouraged the idea that Israel in the period of the judges was a society in a transitional stage between settlement and the establishment of the monarchic state. So, pre-monarchic Israel has in part been interpreted in terms of a semi-nomadic past, and for the rest understood as developing towards the centralized state. That its social structure should be treated as an independent form appropriate to an agricultural non-urban society has not always been adequately recognized. This is especially the case when attention is directed to the question of the nature of the totality of the people Israel, for it has been tempting to adopt as a historical framework of understanding an evolutionary scheme which has at the one end the more or less independent (semi-nomadic) families and clans and at the other the single people organized as a monarchic state; the period of the judges would be then the line holding those two ends together. When the family and clan organization, however, is seen to be no mere survival from the pre-settlement past, but a basic characteristic of a settled, agricultural society, then the form of that society can be given its proper recognition as a distinct and independent social form wholly appropriate to, and meeting the needs of, non-urban Israelite society in the period of the judges.

### c. An Israelite amphictyony

If it is the case that within the pastoral society of Israel the determinative social forms lie at the bottom rather than the top, that it is at the level of the family and the clan that the social and economic form and framework is determined, and that even on the level of the tribe we have come to a secondary and fluid stage of 'tribal' development, we are immediately confronted by a problem: how is 'Israel' to be described in this period? The settings of the deliverers and the minor judges have already been seen to be local rather than national; the widest sphere within which their activities can be understood is a tribal one which does not in itself seem to presuppose the existence of a greater national entity. In what form, then, can we posit 'Israel'? Indeed, it is not beyond the bounds of possibility that the question should be put more radically; can we point to a people 'Israel' in the period of the judges in anything like the form which this entity apparently is understood to have, for example, in the time of Saul? Precisely in this context of the rise of the monarchy the problem becomes quite acute, for the monarchy is widely held to represent an institution alien to the true Israel, which was imposed on this Israel. Israel was something different from the monarchic state, something which was not completely destroyed by the monarchic state, but survived, at least in an attenuated form, as the source of anti-monarchism in Israel. So far, however, we have not identified any people Israel in the pre-monarchic period; rather, the whole drift of the discussion has been towards positing the existence only of fragmented, isolated and un-coordinated rural communities. Was it, then, only with the rise of Saul that these came together, that anything recognizable as a people Israel made its appearance?

We shall be concerned with this issue both here and more positively and extensively in the next chapter. At the present juncture our concern is with a quite distinctive understanding of Israel in the pre-monarchic period, which has had an enormous impact both on our appreciation of the history of the period and indeed also on our conception of the processes which lie behind the origin and development of Israel's tradition, especially that tradition which culminated in the formation of the Pentateuch. When Martin

Noth more than fifty years ago proposed that 'Israel' in the period of the judges was a tribal federation analogous in form to the later classical amphictyony, he gave such convincing and comprehensive expression to what was indeed a quite familiar idea in the scholarly world, that this now became the accepted starting point for more elaborate conceptions and theories. That the classical amphictyony was proposed solely as an analogy was soon forgotten, and it became possible to think of 'the Israelite amphictyony' as a clear datum of Israel's early history. Against this development of the theory, objections such as those raised by Fohrer—that there is no Hebrew equivalent for the Greek amphictyony, that the geographical and historical separation is too great—are indeed effective, but they do not much affect the original proposal, that the classical amphictyony is a suitable analogy by which the early structure of Israel might be understood. In the context of an analogy, the question of influence of one culture upon another simply does not arise; rather, the issue is one of the degree of heuristic value which the analogy has for the purpose for which it is being used. In order to comment adequately on this, we must first describe briefly the theory as it came to classical expression in the work of Noth.

For his reconstruction of Israel in the pre-monarchic period Noth used first and foremost the Old Testament, rather than possible extra-biblical institutions, and here his primary source lay in those texts which consistently present Israel as a people of twelve tribes. Practically all the many lists of sons of Jacob or tribes of Israel retain the number twelve for the total. However, they are not all uniform, and may, in fact, be divided into two basic groups, distinguished by the inclusion or exclusion of the tribe of Levi. This difference has brought others in its train, chief of which is the appearance of Manasseh and Ephraim, instead of the single entity Joseph, in order that the full complement of twelve might be retained in those lists where Levi is absent. Noth understood Num. 26 to be basic to tribal lists of the latter group, and Gen. 49 to be the original listing of sons of Jacob among whom Levi was included. Gen. 49 presents the sons of Jacob as follows: Reuben, Simeon, Levi, Judah, Zebulun, Issachar, Dan, Gad, Asher, Naphtali, Joseph and Benjamin. From the birth story of Gen. 29f. it may be seen that the first six are sons of Leah, the next four are the sons of the handmaids Bilhah and Zilpah, and the last two are sons of Jacob's second wife Rachel. The tribal list of Num. 26, on the other hand, presents the following order: Reuben,

Simeon, Gad, Judah, Issachar, Zebulun, Manasseh, Ephraim, Benjamin, Dan, Asher, Naphtali.

The variations between the lists allow a conclusion to be reached on their relative priority: since it is easier to explain why Levi should have been secondarily omitted from the total rather than why it should have been secondarily included (Levi was originally a secular tribe and, as such, one among the others; at a later stage it was known only as a priestly tribe without land inheritance and so distinct from the others), the list of Gen. 49 must reflect conditions older than those reflected in Num. 26. Both lists, however, are old. Num. 26 establishes this, for among the various families which it assigns to the tribes, several (such as Shechem, Tirzah and Hepher) may be identified as Canaanite city-states of the mountain territories, here reckoned as part of Israel, but none as city states of the plains. The plains of Palestine, at the time of origin of the list, still lay outside Israelite control, a situation which was changed only in the time of David. This means that Num. 26 probably reflects conditions in the pre-monarchic period, and Gen. 49 being older than Num. 26 must also derive from this early time.

In both lists there is consistency in the number twelve of the total; indeed there is also a remarkable consistency in the number six of the 'Leah' group of tribes, for it can only be a concern to maintain that number which can explain the transference of Gad from its proper place in the looser group of 'handmaid' tribes to fill the gap left when Levi was omitted. It is this consistency which requires that we see these lists not as some theoretical idea of Israel but rather as reflecting what was real and historical in the constitution of Israel in the period of the judges.

The Old Testament supplies no adequate historical background and context for an appreciation of the significance of the tribal lists, and so it is at this point that the classical amphictyony is introduced as an appropriate analogy. The amphictyony centered on the two sanctuaries of Apollo at Delphi and of Demeter at Pylae is adopted as the model; about this one most information is preserved, and, indeed as others have noted, it is to this organization that the term 'amphictyony' properly belongs; its application to other organizations in the classical world is already at this stage a deliberately analogous use of the term. According to Noth, the twelve-member structure (or a multiple of twelve) of the amphictyony had a quite practical purpose: each member had the obligation to maintain the sanctuary for a month in the year. It was a loose cultic association in which the sanctuary was the focal point; here representatives of the members would meet regularly, here periodic festivals were held, and such mutual obligations as did bind these members together had reference mainly to the defence and upkeep of the sanctuary.

Noth believed that the foundation of the Israelite amphictyony is recorded in Josh. 24: at Shechem, shortly after the entry of the Yahweh-worshipping house of Joseph into the land, Israel adopted an amphictyonic organization, acknowledging Yahweh as its God and adopting Shechem as its central sanctuary. Here, or at other sanctuaries which seem in turn to have succeeded Shechem, the tribal leaders referred to in Num. 1.5-15 met together. In its common periodic festivals at the sanctuary, Israel worshipped its amphictyonic God Yahweh as its covenant God: it is into a covenant relationship with Yahweh that Joshua introduces amphictyonic Israel in Josh. 24.

For a number of reasons this understanding of pre-monarchic Israel enjoyed very wide popularity. First, it supplied an excellent form by which the nature of pre-monarchic Israel could be described. It had generally been accepted that the essence of Israel and its principle of unity was the worship of Yahweh: it was that which distinguished Israel from the Canaanites. Now, with the amphictyony, the necessary concrete form was given to this otherwise too insubstantial idea. The Israelite amphictyony was a sacral union of the tribes bound together around a common sanctuary in the worship of Yahweh. Remarkably, even those such as Thiel who wish to give up the term 'amphictyony' for Israel all but return to it in their insistence on the necessity for an institutional form within which the community consciousness of Israel, rooted in its common faith in Yahweh, could have come to expression. Yet, at the same time, the amphictyonic structure also explained the lack of political unity so apparent in the traditions from the period of the judges. This was not a political organization, but a sacral one. So, despite the obvious absence of any political structures and of any united political or military action, one could now with all justification refer to the people Israel in the period of the judges.

Secondly, the amphictyony also supplied a context within which it was possible to set institutions and traditions of Israel which were otherwise rootless. Noth himself pointed to the 'minor judges' in Judg. 10.1-5 and 12.7-15 as occupants of an office which had amphictyonic reference: they were judges of amphictyonic Israel, involved perhaps in deciding territorial disputes between the tribes. Other traditions which profited from an amphictyonic background included especially Judg. 19–21, for the internecine war between Benjamin and the rest of Israel described here found a clear parallel in Greek amphictyonic history. However, beyond such isolated traditions, one could also point to the whole Pentateuchal tradition as having experienced its most significant and formative stage of growth within the framework of the amphictyony. It was here that the isolated traditions of the originally independent clans and tribes were brought together, set in order and given a national reference to 'Israel'.

Since the criterion by which this hypothesis is to be judged is the appropriateness of the classical amphictyony as an analogy, it is unnecessary to explore in detail the measure to which this or that individual feature in one context finds a correspondence in the other. In any case, it is often impossible, for lack of evidence, to arrive at any definite conclusion on such possible correspondences. So, the list of tribal leaders in Num. 1.5-15 gives no indication that they performed functions similar to the Greek tribal representatives' task of dealing with the finances of the central sanctuary and acting as a court of arbitration, and, in addition, it seems that those named in Num. 1.5-15 were tribal leaders rather than elected representatives at a collective meeting. This tends to weaken the parallel, but the possibility of using the Greek organization as an analogy is not thereby much diminished.

Remarkably, the same comment may be made on the question of the twelve-tribe constitution of Israel. This is absolutely basic to Noth's thesis, but it has in various studies become clear that none of the tribal lists may clearly be brought back to the pre-monarchic period, that those in the book of Numbers at any rate are most likely priestly constructions, and that even when a list may be earlier it is likely that its function, and the purpose of maintaining the number twelve so consistently, is to express the totality of Israel rather than its precise constitution; as de Vaux has shown, the number twelve was commonly used in order to express totality rather than a numerical significance. However, this does not disqualify the analogy, for it is only to the amphictyony of Delphi that the number twelve originally belonged and even classical writers found no problem in using the term amphictyony of other leagues with seven, twenty-three or eleven members (Strabo 8.6, 14; Thucydides 4.91). It was the idea that each member had to care for the central sanctuary on a regular basis which suggested to Noth the necessity of the number of twelve for the total membership; but in fact in the classical context the obligations of members towards the sanctuary were more likely discharged through their representatives collectively without any monthly rotation of duties among the members. So even here the possibility of the amphictyony standing as a suitable analogy for early Israelite history remains.

Perhaps in the matter of the central sanctuary we have come to a characteristic, if not essential, feature of the amphictyonic organization, so that if a parallel cannot be maintained at this point the analogy is considerably weakened. It is true indeed that questions do arise here, for it was only after having, as he thought, established the validity of the parallel with the classical amphictyony on the basis of the Old Testament tribal lists, that Noth then assumed that Israel too must have had its central sanctuary. This he took to be the ark, and in accordance with its apparent movements through the pre-monarchic period, Noth placed the Israelite central sanctuary in turn at Shechem, Gilgal, Bethel and Shiloh. It is perhaps unnecessary to insist, with Irwin and others, that an Israelite sanctuary cannot be held to have been a central sanctuary unless it was the home of the ark, the place of celebration of the covenant festival between Israel and its amphictyonic God Yahweh, and the meeting place of the tribes or their representatives; these are not criteria derived from the classical amphictyony. However, it must still be acknowledged that while some sanctuaries, such as Gilgal where Saul was anointed king, do seem prominent in early tradition, there is no indication whatever of the formal adoption of such sanctuaries as the responsibility of Israel as a whole. Our confidence in this aspect of the theory is, moreover, even further weakened by a supposed amphictyonic tradition such as that in Judg. 19–21 in which no less than three sanctuaries, Mizpah (20.1), Bethel (20.18) and Shiloh (21.16-21), are concurrently prominent. In this fundamental aspect of the organization the analogy finds no support.

It is, however, on the more general ground of the purpose and function of the amphictyony that its inappropriateness for the Israelite context becomes clearest. It has been shown on several occasions by Noth himself, by Gottwald most recently, and by others, that in the classical context the amphictyony did not form the basis and framework within which a people came into existence.

Rather, it is by an already existing people, which has been brought together by other means and for other reasons, and which is held together by different bonds such as military leagues, that a central sanctuary was adopted and so an amphictyony founded. In the classical context the amphictyony had a purely cultic function. In the Israelite context, however, it has been made to serve not just a cultic function, but a political and ethnic function as well. This is held to have been the context within which Israelite political and ethnic consciousness was shaped. Noth was by no means unaware of the problems, as we can see from his explanation for what he felt to be the rather artificial twelve-tribe scheme, given the fact that it was difficult to point to a time when all twelve tribes and only these twelve tribes existed together as potentially equal partners in an amphictyony. He pointed to a similar artificial organization in Solomon's administrative division of his kingdom into twelve districts to supply the royal court each for one month a year; but if that parallel is to be followed, then its consequence—the prior existence of the people which is organized in this way—must also be admitted. Nevertheless, despite this fundamental problem, the amphictyony remained even for Noth the context within which Israel was thought to have originated and developed.

It seems, therefore, that the classical amphictyony has little heuristic value as an analogy for early Israelite history: quite apart from the substantial points of detail on which it is impossible adequately to justify the analogy, the classical amphictyony cannot by its very nature offer a parallel to the type of political form through which the people Israel could have come to expression in the period of the judges. The amphictyony requires the prior existence of the people. It is the form of the people that we seek, and in the furtherance of this search, the amphictyony offers neither a helpful nor an appropriate analogy. If it can be shown that there was a federation of Israelite tribes in the pre-monarchic period, such as Gottwald has proposed, then we may entertain the possibility that this federation at some stage adopted an amphictyony-like structure, but the latter cannot be made to serve the purpose of the former. It is to this question of the possible existence of a federation of Israelite tribes that we turn in the next chapter.

## For Further Reading

### I

On 'urban' and 'rural' and their relationship:

F.S. Frick, *The City in Ancient Israel* (SBL Dissertation Series, 36; Missoula: Scholars Press, 1977), chs. 1 and 2.

On social structure in Ugarit and Alalakh:

J. Gray, 'Feudalism in Ugarit and Early Israel', *ZAW* 64 (1952), 49-55; I. Mendelsohn, 'Samuel's Denunciation of Kingship in the Light of the Akkadian Documents from Ugarit', *BASOR* 143 (1956), 17-22; A.F. Rainey, 'The Kingdom of Ugarit', *BA* 28 (1965), 102-25; M. Heltzer, *The Rural Community in Ancient Ugarit* (Wiesbaden: Dr Ludwig Reichert Verlag, 1976); A.R.W. Green, 'Social Stratification and Cultural Continuity at Alalakh', *The Quest for the Kingdom of God (Studies in Honor of George E. Mendenhall)* (ed. H.B. Huffmon, F.A. Spina, A.R.W. Green; Winona Lake, Ind.: Eisenbrauns, 1983), 181-203.

### II

On Canaanite society and religion:

A. Alt, 'The Settlement of the Israelites in Palestine', *Essays on Old Testament History and Religion* (Oxford: Blackwell, 1966, and New York: Doubleday, 1967), 133-69; R. de Vaux, *The Early History of Israel* (London: Darton, Longman and Todd, and Philadelphia: Westminster Press, 1978), I, 125-57; N.K. Gottwald, *The Tribes of Yahweh* (New York: Orbis Books, 1979, and London: SCM, 1980), 391-409; K. Koch, 'Zur Entstehung der Baal-Verehrung', *UF* 11 (1979), 465-75; W. Thiel, *Die soziale Entwicklung Israels in vorstaatlicher Zeit* (Neukirchen-Vluyn: Neukirchener Verlag, 1980).

### III

On the Hyksos:

R. de Vaux, *The Early History of Israel* (London: Darton, Longman and Todd, and Philadelphia: Westminster Press, 1978), I, 75-81;

T.O. Lambdin, 'Hyksos', *The Interpreter's Dictionary of the Bible* (Nashville: Abingdon, 1962), II, 667; and J. van Seters, 'Hyksos', *IDB Sup*, 424-25; J.B. Pritchard (ed.), *Ancient Near Eastern Texts Relating to the Old Testament* (Princeton: Princeton University Press; 3rd edn, 1969), 230-34, 554-55.

On the Amarna period:

N.K. Gottwald, *The Tribes of Yahweh* (New York: Orbis Books, 1979, and London: SCM, 1980), 401-409; T.O. Lambdin, 'Tell el-Amarna', *IDB* IV, 529-33; A.F. Rainey, 'Tell el-Amarna', *IDB Sup*, 869; D. Winton Thomas (ed.), *Documents from Old Testament Times* (London: Nelson, 1958), 38-45; J.B. Pritchard (ed.), *Ancient Near Eastern Texts*, 483-90.

On the Habiru:

Gottwald, *The Tribes of Yahweh*, 401-409; de Vaux, *The Early History of Israel*, I, 105-12.


IV

On Israelite social structure:

G.E. Mendenhall, 'The Relation of the Individual to Political Society in Ancient Israel', *Biblical Studies in Memory of H.C. Alleman* (ed. J.M. Myers, O. Reimheer, H.N. Bream; New York: J.J. Augustin, 1960), 89-108; Mendenhall, *The Tenth Generation* (Baltimore: Johns Hopkins, 1973), ch. 1; C.H.J. de Geus, *The Tribes of Israel* (Assen: van Gorcum, 1976), 133-56; W. Thiel, *Die soziale Entwicklung Israels in vorstaatlicher Zeit* (Neukirchen-Vluyn: Neukirchener Verlag, 1980), 88-164; N.K. Gottwald, *The Tribes of Yahweh* (New York: Orbis Books, 1979, and London: SCM, 1980), 239-341.


V

On tribalism and the problem of nomadism:

M.B. Rowton, 'Urban Autonomy in a Nomadic Environment', *JNES* 32 (1973), 201-15; Rowton, 'Autonomy and Nomadism in Western Asia', *Orientalia* 62 (1973), 247-58; C.H.J. de Geus, *The Tribes of Israel* (Assen: van Gorcum, 1976), 124-33; N.K. Gottwald, *The*

*Tribes of Yahweh* (New York: Orbis Books, 1979, and London: SCM, 1980), 435-63: Gottwald, 'Nomadism', *IDB Sup.*, 629-31.

## VI

On the amphictyony:

M. Noth, *Das System der zwölf Stämme Israels* (BWANT IV/1; Stuttgart: Kohlhammer, 1930); Noth, *The History of Israel* (New York: Harper, and London: A. & C. Black, 2nd edn, 1960; reprint London: SCM, 1983), 85-109. The following are the major critical studies: W.H. Irwin, 'Le sanctuaire central israélite avant l'établissement de la monarchie', *RB* 72 (1965), 161-84; G. Fohrer, 'Altes Testament—"Amphiktyonie" und "Bund"', *TLZ* 91 (1966), 801-16, 893-904 (= *Studien zur alttestamentlichen Theologie und Geschichte* [BZAW, 115; Berlin: W. de Gruyter, 1969], 84-119); R. de Vaux, 'La thèse de l'amphictyonie israélite', *HTR* 64 (1971), 415-36 (E.Tr. in *The Early History of Israel* [London: Darton, Longman and Todd, and Philadelphia: Westminster Press, 1978], II, 695-715); A.D.H. Mayes, *Israel in the Period of the Judges* (London: SCM, and Naperville: A.R. Allenson, 1974); C.H.J. de Geus, *The Tribes of Israel* (Assen: van Gorcum, 1976); N.K. Gottwald, *The Tribes of Yahweh* (New York: Orbis Books, 1979, and London: SCM, 1980), 345-57. An exhaustive discussion of the secondary literature is: O. Bächli, *Amphiktyonie im Alten Testament* (Basel: Friedrich Reinhardt Verlag, 1977).

# 3

ISRAEL IN
THE PERIOD OF
THE JUDGES

## A. The Limits of the Period of the Judges

WHAT ARE THE limits of the period of the judges? The end point
is clear enough: the rise of the monarchy. It is true that Saul is
presented to us, in the historically most reliable element of the story
of his rise (1 Sam. 11), as a charismatic leader of the type familiar
from the book of Judges, and so his emergence did not signal an
abrupt end to the period of the judges. Moreover, as we shall indicate
in more detail below, it is erroneous to think in terms of any such
comprehensive transition from rule of the judges to rule of the kings.
The monarchic institution in Israel, for much of its history, caused
less than is usually imagined in the way of fundamental social change
throughout Israel. Its effects were in large measure restricted to the
major urban centres where the king and his court, and, in the case of
the provincial cities, his governors and army commanders, were
located. Rural, tribal Israel would most certainly have felt the effects
of taxation and perhaps to a limited degree the benefits of increasing
prosperity; but its essential way of life, its social structure and tribal
custom, were strongly maintained. Thus, there is a strong element of
continuity between the pre-monarchic and monarchic periods which
makes the rise of Saul a rather artificial break in the account of
Israel's history.

It might at first seem that the starting point presents little
difficulty: the completion of the conquest and occupation of the land,
whether there was a violent conquest, a peaceful process of infiltration,
or a mixture of the two. However, the problems here are, in fact, if
anything greater than those arising from the determination of the end
point of the period of the judges. The biblical presentation of a simple
succession of patriarchs, exodus, wilderness wandering, conquest,
period of the judges is the result of a highly schematic organization of

traditions whose relationship is considerably more complex. The proposition which Noth put forward so forcefully, that the history of Israel begins with the appearance of the tribes in Palestine, is certainly correct, for it is only then that the required conditions of peoplehood: common homeland, common language, and common historical experience, are fulfilled; but it has necessary implications which are not always accepted. Chief among these is the recognition that the traditions of patriarchs, exodus, wilderness wandering, Sinai and conquest represent the creative effort of a people in the land to account for its origins in terms which speak to present conditions and present experience. The patriarchal tradition represents the continuing experience of a family and clan based people with a strong and continuing attachment to the land of Canaan. The exodus tradition reflects the experience of a part of that later Israel whose understanding of Yahweh as deliverer from oppression found such strong echo in the experience of those in the land that Yahweh and his deliverance of the exodus group could be accepted as paradigmatic also for those whose experience had had a quite different form.

This point of view, and the discussion in the last chapter of the nature of semi-nomadism and its relationship with the land, suggest that the nature of Israel's origins should be expressed in these terms: Israel originated in the land of Canaan; the patriarchal traditions reflect an early stage of its life in the land, as a rural, pastoral society, strongly attached to the land but with a semi-nomadic constituent to its way of life; this rural society, nuclear Israel, is not yet in control of the land; the exodus group represents a new and vibrant addition to Israel in the land, bearing a faith in Yahweh as powerful deliverer of the oppressed; this faith forcefully reflected the developing experience also of tribal Israel in its relationship with the city-states of Canaan, so that the exodus could easily be claimed as a valid expression of the faith even of those who had no direct link with it. Israel and the people of Yahweh are not synonymous terms; Israel, as its name indicates, was at the first a people of El; with the integration of the exodus group, however, Israel became the people of Yahweh, and, under the influence of its new-found faith, its tradition both absorbed, and was itself re-shaped by, the exodus tradition of the new arrivals in the land.

In this light, the period of the judges cannot be said simply to start with the entry into the land by those who came out of Egypt at the exodus. Rather, it is a period which reaches right back behind that event, which itself represents in part the arrival of newcomers into the land and in part the continuation of that process by which rural Israel in Canaan gradually won control of the land. The period of the judges is thus not to be comprehended by some more or less arbitrary dates, 1200 BC or thereabouts being taken as the time of the conquest, and 1020 BC or thereabouts being taken as the date of Saul's accession. These dates, and the events to which they point, represent stages in a much more comprehensive process which is the essence of the period of the judges.

This process is that by which power in Canaan was transferred from the individual and independent city-states, located mainly in the coastal plain and the plain of Esdraelon, to rural, tribal elements which were located in the main in the mountain territories free of city-state control. It is a process which culminated in the creation under David of a single independent power structure in Canaan, one which continued to have its base on the mountains. This is in broad outline the context within which the period of the judges belongs, though it is by no means to be understood as a single, unified process. The stream is a broad one, and the currents which comprise it are very varied, not all pulling in one direction, and by no means all aimed at the one conclusion, the rise of the Israelite monarchy. This will become clear in a provisional way in the next section. Yet, in general, this outline can be accepted as marking the limits within which the period of the judges lies and the broad background against which the events of the period are to be understood.

## B. Israel as a Segmentary Society in the Period of the Judges

Surely one very radical question arises from our discussion so far: on what grounds can we speak of 'Israel' at all in the period of the judges? Our literary study has shown that the book of Judges breaks down into a number of independent traditions which tell of local heroes and local events; our study of tribal society has indicated that the basic social unit is the extended family, a number of which are banded together in the clan, but that the tribe is a vague and insubstantial entity which has little concrete reality in the form of given social structure. The reality of a social entity 'Israel' in the period of the judges must then be open to question.

The very considerable advantage of Noth's proposal of the amphictyony as an analogy for pre-monarchic Israel was that it provided precisely the means of maintaining the real existence of an Israel in the period of the judges, which could be identified as the context of origin of institutions and traditions which, for one reason or another, were considered to be early. Gottwald's massive treatment of the pre-monarchic period dismissed the usefulness of the analogy of the amphictyony, but could not give up the need for a tribal federation called Israel. He effectively identified two grounds for requiring an 'Israel' in the period of the judges. In the first place, there is the common tribal structure which characterizes the people, and thus is held to presuppose some comprehensive organizational framework; secondly, there is the common Israelite consciousness which comes to expression in so much of Israel's tradition, especially that of the Pentateuch. Neither of these, however, is conclusive: the tribal structure which Gottwald describes was a feature probably also of peoples on Israel's borders, especially Edomites, Moabites and Ammonites, so Israel's tribal structure cannot be held to be exclusive and so to presuppose some social structure comprehending just those tribes which are identified as Israelite. Secondly, the background of the 'Israel' presupposed by the Pentateuchal tradition is no longer so clearly a pre-monarchic Israel; Gottwald relies here very strongly on an approach to Pentateuchal criticism, developed by Noth and von Rad, which pointed to the pre-monarchic time as that in which the old traditions were first brought into systematic order. However, so many problems now surround questions of the time of origin and arrangement of the Pentateuchal traditions that this can no longer serve as a sure basis for positing an 'Israel' in the period of the judges.

On the face of it, the monarchy appears to be that form through which Israel as a social reality actually came into existence; only with the monarchy was that super-tribal structure provided which held the whole together as a single people. However, it is, in fact, no real solution to the problem to think in terms of an evolving unit which only became a single entity, Israel, at the time of the foundation of the monarchy. Such a developmental view posits the monarchy as an inevitable result of unifying forces at work within a gradually evolving Israel, rather than as an institution which an existing tribal people felt constrained to adopt, in large part because of the exigencies of external pressure and threats posed by Ammonites and Philistines. It is only a superficially attractive view, and really presupposes a much too simplistic understanding of the relationship between Israel and the monarchic state. The latter did not emerge as an Israelite social system in succession to and bringing together disparate tribal elements which had hitherto had nothing which could be described as 'peoplehood'. Gottwald has developed a useful model by which a framework of understanding of the origin of the monarchic state and its relationship to Israel may be appreciated. It is an institution which serves economic and military purposes, creating structures by which economic resources may be better exploited to the benefit of all and military resources organized for common defence. It has, however, an inherent centralizing tendency which develops its own momentum, so that, ceasing to serve the needs of the people, it comes to serve its own ends, becoming finally alienated from those for whose benefit it was originally established.

This is a useful way in which to view the Israelite situation for two reasons: first, it maintains the essential distinction between the people 'Israel' and the monarchic state as a structure superimposed on that people; secondly, it allows an investigation of pre-monarchic Israel from a standpoint which is not governed solely by the need to find centralizing tendencies or unifying trends within the people. Undoubtedly the monarchic state has roots within Israel as well as external causes, but these roots do not necessarily constitute the essence of the nature of pre-monarchic Israel. This older Israel continued into the monarchic period, its life and customs often unaffected by the monarchic institution; the latter developed and institutionalized one form of pre-monarchic leadership in Israel, but did not express what was essentially characteristic of tribal Israel. Pre-monarchic tribal Israel was a society in its own right and is not to be seen solely as preparatory to the monarchy.

If, then, it is right to think of a people 'Israel' in the period of the judges some attempt must be made to give it concrete description. This is not achieved simply through pointing to Israel's faith in Yahweh, for to say that Israel was the people of Yahweh, true in a limited sense as that might be, is not to offer a definition of the people Israel as a social unit.

Moreover, such a proposal probably presupposes a mistaken understanding of the role of religion in society, since, although a common religion will certainly serve as a strong unifying and binding influence, religion as such expresses an already existing identity and does not provide the basis and foundation for that identity. Noth held that Israel's faith was its distinctive characteristic, but he considered that religion for this period meant the amphictyonic cult and this was a religious institution created for particular purposes on given 'raw material'; thus, even for Noth the amphictyonic structure was a secondary formation. So even if that analogy is still to be held in some very limited way, it is necessary to provide some account of the nature of the 'raw material' within which it functioned.

De Geus has introduced two terms which are descriptively appropriate in this connection: *connubium* and *forum*. By *connubium* is meant the intermarriage of Israelites within a particular social context which then forms the limits of the people; by *forum* is meant the context within which certain norms of behaviour are accepted. It is within the context of the people alone that marriage is acceptable, and, as Num. 25.1 indicates, any marriage outside that framework is considered 'whoredom'. In a similar way, the tradition of Gen. 34 reflects the belief that only after Canaanite Shechem had been united with Israel into 'one people' could intermarriage take place (vv. 16, 22). It must be noted, of course, in view of our earlier discussion of the significance of the endogamous clan, that intermarriage and blood relationship are a reality at the clan level of society, so that when Israel as a whole is described in blood relationship terms, this is the fictional application of terminology which really applied only with the clan: Israel is a group of endogamous clans. Thus, *connubium* on its own cannot offer a historical account of Israel since in practice it is a feature of the life of the clan rather than of the people which is a number of such clans.

The observance of a common code of moral and ethical behaviour is the second significant determinant of a society, and in this connection the phrase *nᵉbālâ bᵉyiśrā'ēl*, 'folly in Israel', is of particular importance. It is usually used of the violation of a code of sexual behaviour (Gen. 34.7; Deut. 22.21; Judg. 20.6; 2 Sam. 13.12; Jer. 29.23), though it had more general application (Josh. 7.15). This is clearly a formula, and not just an *ad hoc* expression for a particular crime. It presupposes the existence of a given order, an accepted code of conduct, which, in the particular action for which the formula has been used, has been grossly violated. Quite clearly, the regular appearance of the term 'Israel' in conjunction with 'folly' in this formula indicates that this code goes beyond the limits of the extended family, clan and tribe, to embrace a much wider society, and a society whose very existence is in large measure determined by its acquiescence to the way of life which this formula presupposes. The concrete norms which defined this way of life, and the violation of which is considered 'folly in Israel', cannot be determined with any certainty; but insofar as the collection of laws contained in the so-called 'Book of the Covenant' in Ex. 20.23–23.33 cannot possibly be identified as state law, supported by the authority of the king, it gives every impression of being a definition of conduct accepted by and determining the limits of pre-monarchic Israel.

The kind of society presupposed here, characterized by a common tribal structure in which marriage took place within the clan, and by the common acceptance of a certain code of conduct, was not a tightly knit group open to clear formal definition and description. It was a very loosely structured society, subject to considerable internal change over time. Gottwald's attempt to describe a fairly clearly delimited group, identifiable not just on the basis of a common tribal structure and a common Israelite consciousness, but more precisely as a group held together by what he calls 'cross-cutting associations', is in the end not really successful. The extent to which groups like the Levites and the popular army functioned to hold together a number of independent clans or tribes is completely unclear, and we can at best think of them as quite secondary links existing within an already established social context, rather than as associations which themselves constitute the basis of that society's existence. This is not to say that such associations did not function above the clan or tribal level, for it is very probable that, for example, the clan functioned to raise troops for the popular army in the context of a wider responsibility shared by other clans and tribes to do the same; or again, faith in Yahweh is not identifiable as the religion of any particular clan, and this also then formed a bond, perhaps expanded and maintained by levites, between groups which had no kinship links. However, in neither case is it possible to point to characteristic traits which marked off a particular number of clans and tribes as Israel. These associations operate within limits loosely established on other grounds and do not themselves set those limits.

The tribal lists which we examined in the last chapter are no more helpful here. The dating of them is a complex and uncertain question which cannot be discussed here; but even if that most unlikely theory, that they come from the pre-monarchic period, is to be entertained, they still reveal little in the way of a constitution for Israel in the period of the judges. They bring together traditional tribal entities with actually existing tribes, and they combine different traditional groups of tribes, with the purpose of giving expression to the totality of Israel. They do not presuppose an actual Israel corresponding to the contents of these lists, but point to various attempts to define the whole from different points of view, while giving due weight to both traditional and existing conditions. The twelve of the number of the tribes expresses the totality 'Israel', and does not necessarily correspond to its actual composition at any given period.

It is this very fluid picture of Israel in the period of the judges which encourages confidence in a more recent analogy which has been proposed for Israel, especially by Malamat, Crüsemann and Lohfink: the 'segmentary society' exemplified by some African tribal societies. Among the African peoples characterized by this social form are the Nuer with a population of some 300,000 and an economic base in agriculture and livestock. Society consists of a number of uniform clans within larger tribal groupings. There is no central authority and the place of the individual in society is genealogically defined. Authority is exercised most effectively at the lowest level in the person of the family father; there are also village elders who have, however, no power to enforce their decisions. In time of crisis leadership is exercised by individuals, sometimes of a prophetic type, who gain a following which goes beyond the tribe, but whose position lasts only for the duration of the crisis which called it forth.

Such a social form does not represent the temporary structure assumed by a society on the way to becoming a unified, centralized state; rather, it is a quite independent form of social organization. Its correspondence with Israel in the pre-monarchic period is remarkably close: in both cases, one is dealing with a society based on agriculture and livestock; in both, it is an egalitarian society with authority exercised chiefly at the lowest level of the family; in both, genealogical systems are of basic importance as the means by which the place of the individual in society and his relationship to others might be determined; in both, there is a charismatic type of leadership which goes beyond the tribe in times of crisis; in both, there is a remarkable uniformity and coherence, and an ability to resist external pressures despite the lack of structural unity and a central authority. Above all, both contexts are characterized by the fact that the lack of state organization, which expresses itself in centrally organized authority and power, is no barrier to the existence of a common consciousness, a sense in the individual and the clan of belonging to the people.

There are certainly points where the corresponcence is not apparent, perhaps especially in the lack of an African parallel to Israel's common worship of Yahweh; but the analogy is nevertheless an impressive one. It does not exclude the possibility of smaller amphictyony-like leagues within society, but, more importantly, it does not require that one should think in terms of such a league as comprehending the total society, and as necessary for that society's self-understanding as a people. The existence of Israel in the period of the judges may, on the strength of this analogy, be accepted even though its peoplehood found no institutional expression.

## C. Leadership in Pre-monarchic Israel

### a. Charismatic leadership

i. *The wars of Israel*

The events related in the stories of deliverance in the book of Judges fit perfectly in the context of an Israel understood on the analogy of the segmentary socity: although composed of independent units, its social divisions could be overcome by charismatic leadership in crisis situations. The traditions brought together in the original collection of deliverer stories are a good illustration of the variety possible in the extent to which any particular charismatic leader commanded support from the clans and tribes. The Ehud story of Judg. 3.12-30 presupposes a situation where the Moabites had expanded far beyond their own territory east of the Dead Sea and south of the Arnon. Apparently supported by Ammonites and Amalekites (indeed probably having subdued Ammonites and Amalekites), the Moabites established their frontier with Israel at the lower parts of the Jordan, a situation presupposed also in the Balaam stories in Num. 22–24 and also in Num. 25.1-5. Their attempt to extend their control west of the Jordan, occupying Jericho and forcing the Benjaminites to pay them tribute, eventually provoked a reaction: the Benjaminite Ehud killed Eglon the king of Moab and, with the help of Ephraimites summoned to his aid, destroyed the Moabite garrison and expelled the Moabites back east of the Jordan, to restore what was apparently considered the normal state of affairs.

The second episode, the victory of Deborah and Barak over Sisera (Judg. 4–5), was of a different nature. This was no repulsion of neighbours attempting to encroach on Israelite territory, but rather a tribal victory over the declining city-state system within Palestine. The name Sisera has been linked with the Sea Peoples, a link which would imply the involvement of the Philistines with the kings of Canaan as Israel's foes. That link is not impossible: the Philistines are known to have been at Bethshean (cf. 1 Sam. 31), and the Philistine city-state system was no different from the indigenous Canaanite system in representing a social structure in process of losing control of the land before the rising power of tribal Israel.

The immediate cause of the conflict is not clear: perhaps Judg. 5.6 indicates Canaanite disruption of the highways connecting Israelite tribal areas. However, its result was a victory for tribal Israel which marked a significant development in the area of its control and influence in Palestine. The battle was won 'at Taanach by the waters of Megiddo' (Judg. 5.19), and the victory ensured Israelite control of the strategically vital plain of Esdraelon.

The alliance of tribes under the leadership of Barak was considerably wider than that which Ehud mustered: on this occasion not only Ephraim and Benjamin, but also Machir, Zebulon, Issachar, and perhaps also Naphtali, came together (Judg. 5.13-15 [18]), while the poet in the Song of Deborah saw no good reason for the absence of Reuben, Gilead, Dan and Asher, peripheral tribes from Galilee and east Jordan. It is not necessary to think that a ten-tribe federation as such is presupposed here; this was a single occasion of common action, and does not necessarily reflect an alliance which had other political, social or cultic forms of expression. What is certainly remarkable, however, is the absence of any reference to Judah and Simeon, and it is reasonable to assume that the common Israelite consciousness of this period did not extend to these southern tribes. It is insufficient to refer in this connection to the fact that Canaanite city-states separated Judah and Simeon from the other tribes, for it is clear that 'Israel' as far as the traditions of Judges are concerned (with the exception of the late and quite individual tradition of Othniel in Judg. 3.7-11), was located mainly in central west Jordan, extending also to Galilee and into east Jordan. The Judean area, which even later shows its distinctiveness from the others, does not come within its view.

The remaining tradition of the old collection, the Gideon–Abimelech story in Judg. 6–9, has undergone considerable development which makes the historical background very difficult to reconstruct. The emergency which Gideon came forward to meet was Midianite raiding of Israelite land at harvest time, apparently a regular occurrence which affected especially the Manassites, to whom Gideon's clan of Abiezer belonged. With a small band, probably consisting of Abiezrites only, Gideon mounted a sudden attack on the Midianite camp at the south-western end of the plain of Jezreel, and sent them in panic-stricken flight back across the Jordan. The extent of Israelite involvement is quite uncertain, and the tradition itself shows no uniformity on the matter (compare Judg. 6.34f. and 7.23); most probably it involved Gideon with his own clan only, while the later telling of the story has introduced other tribes, whose living in the vicinity would have been understood to have implied their involvement. This, like the Ehud story, was a local event with a local hero achieving a notable victory.

The Abimelech story appended secondarily to the Gideon tradition has affinities more with the Deborah–Barak tradition than with that of Gideon, for, as with the Sisera episode, here again it is a question of Israelite relations with the city-state society in Palestine. The story is a good illustration of the fact that the borders between tribal and city-state society were not clear cut; the development of Israelite tribalism took place in the context of various types of relationship with the city-states. On this occasion, an attempt on the part of Abimelech, having made himself a city-state king, to extend his rule into the tribal area of Manasseh and create a sphere of influence of considerable extent, ended in failure, the destruction of Shechem and his own death. This seems to have represented an attempt to restore a style of government in Shechem and its environment which is known from the Amarna period. Reviv has shown the close parallels which exist between the two periods: Labayu in the Amarna period was, like Abimelech later, a foreigner who was hired by the lords of Shechem at a time when the city was an enclave requiring protection. However, with the destruction of Shechem, which may archaeologically be dated to the twelfth century, this early attempt to establish monarchy in the heart of tribal Israel was brought to an end.

The old collection of deliverer stories was gradually supplemented: at different times the stories of Othniel (Judg. 3.7-11), Jephthah (Judg. 10.6–12.6), Samson (Judg. 13–16) and the note on Shamgar (Judg. 3.31) have been added. Of these, the formulaic nature of the Othniel story and the brevity of the note on Shamgar allow no conclusions to be drawn on any historical background; the story of Samson is the story of an individual champion rather than of a charismatic leader; it is really only the Jephthah account which as a type conforms with the other deliverer stories. The Jephthah incident presupposes expansion by the Ammonites to the north-west, which brought them into conflict with the Gileadites settled in east Jordan. To meet that danger the elders of Gilead hired Jephthah, appointing him as their 'head', and he, with a band of adventurers of whom he was already leader, repulsed the Ammonites from Gileadite territory. The lack of reliable site identifications for the places mentioned as the scene of the battle in Judg. 11.33 makes it impossible to be clear about the extent of Jephthah's victory, but it should probably be seen as in general a defensive action more concerned with driving Ammonites out of Gilead than with extending Gileadite influence beyond its established borders. It was certainly a local event and gave rise to a local tradition handed down independently; only at a late stage was it connected with the collection of deliverer stories, which was concerned with events mainly in central western Palestine.

## ii. *Holy war and charisma*

These wars of the pre-monarchic period are usually described as holy wars led by charismatic deliverers. This is a description which should be used only with some qualification. Von Rad described the holy war as a cultic institution of the amphictyony, which had certain regular features: the participants were summoned through the blowing of the trumpet, certain taboos were observed, sacrifice was offered, formulaic language was used (for example 'Yahweh has delivered your enemies into your hands', 'return to your tents, O Israel'). It was an event in which Yahweh himself participated, spreading panic among the enemy. The later studies of Smend, Stolz and Jones have, however, modified this picture considerably. No amphictyonic association ever appears in this connection: there is no uniform pattern; and this is no more a sacred institution than any significant event in the experience of the people and the individual. It is only with the deuteronomic school that a theory or theology of holy war is developed, and it is this essentially deuteronomic theoretical pattern which has erroneously been taken as the model by which Israel's ancient wars were conducted. One may perhaps better describe these wars as wars of Yahweh and reserve the designation 'holy war' for the schematic presentation of the tradition in the framework of deuteronomic theology. To refer to these wars, however, under any single designation carries the risk of stereotyping them in a

way which is not true to the events in the earliest tradition about
them.

The description of the war leaders in the period of the judges as
'charismatics' goes back to Weber's application of the term charisma
to one model of authority or leadership which existed alongside two
other forms: traditional authority (such as that exercised by the
elders), and legal authority (the monarchy). Weber was concerned
more with prophets than with the pre-monarchic deliverer, but the
application of the term to the latter has become common. It has been
developed especially by Malamat who sees charismatic leadership as
in part a response to a situation where traditional authority in clan
and tribe is in process of dissolution, while the centralized established leadership of the monarchy has not yet emerged. Charismatic
authority was spontaneous, exclusive and personal, temporary and
completely independent of established social forms and instruments
of authority; its appearance is the result of the coalescence of a
particular personality with a particular set of circumstances, a
potential leader at a time of enduring major crisis. This is a good
description, but once again a certain caution is necessary. Some
aspects of the presentation of the deliverers in the oldest collection
probably owe much to a prophetic context of transmission of
tradition, in which it is the type of inspired prophetic leader which is
projected back on the older deliverers. Moreover, both Ehud and
Jephthah were already leaders in different ways, and the extent to
which their authority can be described as spontaneous and arising
only out of the crisis of the moment is uncertain. In general, these
wars were local conflicts, in which the form of leadership which
emerged varied according to the circumstances of time and place.

**b. The minor judges**
Within the segmentary society of Israel the authority of the family
father was fundamental. He had the responsibility for the ordering of
life in all its aspects within the basic element of society, the extended
family. His power over his family was absolute: he could sell his
children into slavery (Ex. 21.7), sacrifice them to preserve his own
honour (Gen. 19.8; Judg. 19.24), and even make life and death
decisions concerning them (Gen. 38.24; 42.37); this extreme authority
was diminished only relatively late, when it was apparently transferred to a court constituted by the elders of the district (Deut. 21.18-
21). The elders were a body probably at least originally comprising

the family fathers of a district, to whom would be referred issues beyond the competence or concern of the family father acting alone. They had a judicial role, but in addition a representative or governing role. It was the elders of Gilead who negotiated the terms under which Jephthah would take the power to deal with the threat posed by the Ammonites (Judg. 11.4ff.); it was to the elders of Judah that David sent spoil from his raids, undoubtedly with a view to his own future leadership (1 Sam. 30.26ff.).

In such a society, what then could have been the role of those who ✳ in Judg. 10.1-5 and 12.7-15 are said to have 'judged Israel'? There are six of these so-called minor judges, and the record in Judges is undoubtedly a formal document which has only secondarily been broken by the insertion of the story about Jephthah; that insertion was made at the point where the name of Jephthah occurred as one of those in the list who 'judged Israel'. The connection between judge and deliverer which appears with Jephthah does not necessarily hold for any other deliverer; Jephthah's is a unique case which does not affect the general point that the list of minor judges should be considered independently of the stories of deliverers in questions of its background and historical reference. Noth carried out a major study of this list, and even though his interpretation of it as a formal record of those who occupied an amphictyonic office of 'judge of Israel' can scarcely now be maintained, his basic recognition of the independence of the list remains valid.

That recognition must, in principle, be emphasized, especially in the light of the various attempts of Hertzberg, Schunck and Malamat to break down the differences between minor judges and deliverers. Malamat does this in historical terms by arguing that the verb ✳ translated 'judge' has a much wider meaning, comprehending also the leadership activities of the deliverers, so that the difference between major and minor judges resides in the nature of the sources used rather than in any distinction in the historical situation referred to in those sources. The question of the meaning of the verb 'judge' we shall revert to later. Hertzberg and Schunck, on the other hand, attempt to cope with the literary problem. The list of minor judges contains certain constant features: each judge is connected with his predecessor by the words 'after him', of each it is said that he judged Israel for a certain number of years, and of each his death and place of burial are recorded. If any connection is to be established between the minor judges and individuals referred to outside the list of Judg.

10.1-5 and 12.7-15, then some link must be found with this literary scheme. Schunck proposes, by establishing such a link, to supplement the list of six minor judges with the names of Joshua, Othniel, Ehud, Gideon, Samson and Samuel; Hertzberg with the names of Othniel, Deborah, Gideon, Abimelech, Eli and Samuel. In each case the number twelve of the total (itself a significant number in the Israelite context) is attained.

However, such literary references as there are to link these additional figures to the list of minor judges are in general fragmentary. Samuel has the strongest connection, since of him it is related in 1 Sam. 7.15 that 'he judged Israel all the days of his life', and 1 Sam. 25.1 that he 'died . . . and they buried him in his house at Ramah'; it could, furthermore, be argued that the first constant of the literary form used for the minor judge, the words 'after him', by which each was connected to his predecessor, has, in the case of Samuel as also in that of Jephthah, been suppressed as a result of the incorporation of other material and the resulting separation of the individual from his position in the list. On the other hand, the literary linking of the other figures to the list of minor judges is too slight to withstand scrutiny: in several cases, as with Deborah (Judg. 4.4) and Eli (1 Sam. 4.18), the link is a minor one and also probably a late addition, from a deuteronomistic (or later) hand; in others, as with Othniel (Judg. 3.10f.), the link is more impressive, but is certainly, as we saw in Chapter 1, the deliberate work of an editor who is consciously forging a link between the minor judges and the deliverers. There is no real argument for supplementing the list of minor judges in Judg. 10.1-5 and 12.7-15 with any individual other than Samuel.

A major study of the list which has contributed much to our understanding of its literary presentation and background has been carried out by Richter. While Noth argued persuasively for its antiquity and integrity, Richter has concentrated on what he considers to be signs of redactional work within the list. Thus, the fact that in Judg. 10.1, 3 the verb 'arose' appears, while Judg. 12.7, 8, 11, 13 use 'judged', is taken as an unevenness pointing to the work of a later redactor; on the other hand, the schematic nature of the list is also taken to indicate the hand of an editor at work on handed-down material. The judges are generally said to have functioned out of cities rather than tribes, which would indicate that the 'Israel' which they judged was one in which the tribes were secondary to the cities from the point of view of social structure and organization; this was not the case in the pre-monarchic period. Thus, the list relates to a historical reality of the pre-monarchic period only in a very broken and incomplete way; in important respects, particularly in the reference to 'Israel' and the presentation of the judges as acting in succession, it reflects a much later time.

Richter goes on to compare the scheme of the list of minor judges with that used for the kings of Israel and Judah, including Saul (1 Sam. 13.1), David (1 Kings 2.10-12) and Solomon (1 Kings 11.41-43). The royal scheme contains statements on the length of the individual king's reign, the area over which he ruled, his death and place of burial, and the accession of his successor. Clearly the forms used for judges and kings are related, and, according to Richter, one should think in terms of the dependence of the former on the latter: the scheme used for the judges can be explained much more easily as an imitation of that used for the kings than can the royal scheme be explained as secondarily dependent on that used for the judges. The 'Israel' to which the scheme for the judges refers is, therefore, the Israel of the monarchic period, the northern kingdom.

In at least one fundamental respect Richter is probably correct here: it is highly probable that the presentation of the judges in Judg. 10.1-5 and 12.7-15 as judging Israel in strict succession should be seen as the result of an attempt to represent government in pre-monarchic Israel as analogous to the form it adopted under the monarchy. The Samuel tradition confirms this in two respects. First of all, the Samuel tradition, in 1 Sam. 7.15 and 25.1, as already noted, ᵗis closely connected with the list of judges; yet, in that tradition there is no reference to Samuel's having succeeded a predecessor; the element of succession can, therefore, be taken as not having formed part of the basic tradition of the judges. Secondly, while Samuel is indeed said to have 'judged Israel', just as did the minor judges, the tradition elaborates on this (1 Sam. 7.16f.) by saying that 'he went on a circuit year by year to Bethel, Gilgal and Mizpah; and he judged Israel in all these places. Then he would come back to Ramah, for his home was there, and there also he administered justice to Israel.' Samuel was clearly a judge in the area of the mid-Palestinian tribes of Ephraim and Benjamin, a local figure whose sphere of activity was confined to areas not far removed from his home. This must also have been the case with those judges mentioned in Judg. 10.1-5 and 12.7-15, and if so, then the idea that they succeeded one another should be seen as resulting from a secondary, and unnecessary, interpretation of the meaning of 'Israel'. The latter need not be taken as the northern kingdom, as Richter has understood it; but, as in the Samuel tradition, it can be taken to refer to the tribal people Israel within which Samuel acted as judge in Ephraim and Benjamin. Thus, the judges of the list may well have been in some cases contemporaries.

Furthermore, Richter's argument that the list presupposes conditions in which the city is primary and the tribe secondary is only to a limited extent true; it is not true in the sense that the list presupposes a monarchic rather than pre-monarchic background. Cities were not strange to pre-monarchic Israel, and the preference for relating the judges to cities rather than tribes is probably a reflection of the nature of the work of the judge rather than of any general priority of cities over tribes. Thus, the argument of Noth for the antiquity and integrity of the list of judges can be held to stand except for one (and indeed one important) point: their presentation as successive judges is a reflection of monarchic succession in Israel of a later time; otherwise, in the names, periods of office and locations, there is good reason to hold to the historical reliability of this list.

The functions performed by these judges remain clouded by obscurity. Alt proposed, on the basis of an Icelandic parallel, that they were the mediators to newly settled Israel of the casuistic law of Canaan, which Israel had to adopt after her occupation of the land. Noth suggested a function appropriate to the amphictyony, within which considered the judge to have had a central role: they proclaimed to the assembled Israelites the amphictyonic law. These judges were occupants of a central amphictyonic office which was so significant for Israel that it was maintained even after the introduction of the monarchy (Deut. 17.8-13; Mic. 5.1 [4.14 in the Hebrew]). Others, however, have made use of the fact that cognates of the verb *špṭ*, usually translated 'judge', have in other Semitic languages the more general sense of 'rule' or 'govern', besides the specific sense of 'judge'; and those named in Judg. 10.1-5 and 12.7-15 have been understood, therefore, as 'rulers', perhaps in an urban rather than a tribal context, whose function included not only judicial but also civic, administrative duties. De Vaux has surveyed the different usages of the verb in Phoenician and Punic, Ugaritic and in the Mari texts, and has quite clearly demonstrated that the wider sense of 'rule' or 'govern' is required in many examples. However, despite his conclusion that the same holds good for the Israelite case, and that the judges were then 'an instrument of government', an element of doubt must remain. The overwhelming majority of usages of the word in Hebrew are judicial, and only very few, such as 2 Kings 15.5, require the more general sense. Moreover, it is possible that the sense of 'rule' or 'govern' represents a meaning of the word only in a state context, and is not a primary sense which can easily be carried over from that state context to the situation of pre-monarchic Israel.

If this is so, and the judicial sense of the verb should then be preferred for Judg. 10.1-5 and 12.7-15, it does not necessarily follow that there was some duplication of the functions of the family father or the elders; nor does it follow that such a judge served as some sort of court of appeal, a court for which, in this early period, there is indeed no reliable evidence. There is a different kind of function which they may have served, one which is suggested by analogy from the later role of the Israelite king, by one aspect of the list of judges itself, and by the general context of Israel in the pre-monarchic period. This is that they were mediators between different traditions of law and custom in the tribal society of Israel, in the context of the general process of evolution of a uniform legal tradition. It is that role which is presupposed for the king in 2 Sam. 14, where the conflict between the right of the avenger of blood and the right of the family to posterity must be resolved; the list of judges itself suggests this as a possible function in that it presents the judges generally without particular tribal affiliation, and so as potential mediators in disputes between tribes; it is, finally, such a function which must have become a necessity in a segmentary society characterized by the independence of its tribal constituents. This role suits not only the list of judges in Judg. 10.1-5 and 12.7-15, but also the specific case of Samuel in 1 Sam. 7.15-17.

## D. The History of Israel in the Period of the Judges

### a. The chronology of the period of the judges

Noth argued that the minor judges historically had great significance for pre-monarchic chronology. They were the bearers of a central Israelite amphictyonic office, according to whose year in office events would have been dated. Thus, even if the activities of the deliverers could not easily be related to the minor judges, it would in theory have been possible to establish at least some sort of skeletal chronology of the period, however incomplete. However, we have seen that just this aspect of the list of minor judges, their presentation as successive occupants of an office, is probably a secondary characteristic reflecting monarchic conditions; the judges were not occupants of a central office, but were local figures who in many cases may well have been contemporaries. The years they spent in office cannot therefore be used in order to construct any chronology of Israel's history in this period.

Despite the potential usefulness of the minor judges in this respect, it has, in fact, generally been on the basis of the stories of the wars of Israel, with foes both within and from outside the land, that a particular order of events has been proposed. The very order in which these battles are related in the book of Judges has been seen as significant in this regard, and indeed it is certainly possible to develop a certain historical logic from that order. Thus, the Ehud story in Judg. 3.12-30 presupposes the expansion of Moab right up to the area of the Jordan river just north of the Dead Sea; but the story makes no reference to Gad or Reuben, Israelite tribes which are at other times known to have been settled in that part of southern Transjordan which Judg. 3 presupposes to have been occupied by the Moabites. In the Moabite Stone, from the mid-ninth century BC, the Moabite king Mesha refers to the men of Gad having been settled in the land of Ataroth, about eight miles north of the Arnon, 'from of old', and in Num. 33.45f. the city of Dibon, just three miles north of the Arnon, is described as Dibon-gad. The tribe of Reuben is more difficult to locate, since some references (Josh. 15.6; 18.17) seem to presuppose a memory of its having lived west of Jordan; however, the tribal territorial descriptions always mention Reuben in close connection with Gad (Num. 32.1ff.; Josh. 13.15ff.), and so its location in east Jordan is a much more likely probability, whatever its origin may have been. In both cases it is impossible to be sure about the times to which the various references relate, but there is no reason for dating the presence of Gad in its familiar territory later than the premonarchic period. Thus, the Ehud tradition seems to presuppose early conditions, and so stands appropriately at the beginning of the stories of deliverers.

The victory of Deborah and Barak over Sisera has no clear connection with the Ehud incident; but it could be argued that on

this occasion Israel's defeat of the kings of Canaan in the plain of
Jezreel and their consequent destruction of the Canaanite defences in
this area created the conditions which allowed incursions from the
desert by Midianites, Amalekites and 'peoples of the east', which
form the background to the Gideon story. It could be argued further
that this order of events is supported by the references to Manasseh
in the Gideon tradition (Judg. 6.35; 7.23), for these presuppose a
situation later than the Song of Deborah, which refers to Machir
(Judg. 5.14), rather than Manasseh; it seems that Machir was the
older tribal entity which, for some unknown reason, migrated in large
part to east Jordan, leaving behind an element which adopted the
name Manasseh. Moreover, the references in the Gideon tradition to
Manasseh, Asher, Zebulon and Naphtali (Judg. 6.35; 7.23) could be
taken as an indication that the Gideon battle presupposed a freedom
of action on the part of those tribes which could only have followed
on the victory of Deborah and Barak over Sisera and the kings of
Canaan.

The Jephthah tradition is a secondary accretion to the old book of
deliverers, as we have already seen, and this in itself makes it highly
improbable that any historical significance is to be assigned to the
simple fact that it appears where it does after the Gideon (–
Abimelech) story. It could nevertheless be argued that the rise of
Ammon and its threat to the security of Gilead, which stands behind
the Jephthah story, could not have taken place without Gideon's
defeat of the Midianites, and particularly without Ehud's defeat of
the Moabites. So also the place of the Jephthah tradition in relation
to the others has a certain historical logic: only with the decline of
Moab was the rise and expansion of Ammon possible.

In general, however, all such arguments are very speculative, and
it is impossible to create a reliable chronology of the period of the
judges on their basis. The Ehud tradition centres on that individual
and his heroic victory over Eglon, and not much significance can
possibly be attached to its lack of reference to Gad and Reuben.
Again, there is nothing certain about the argument that Midianite
raids in Jezreel could only have taken place after Israel's defeat of
Sisera and the kings of Canaan. Those raids were just that, and could
have taken place just as easily before that Israelite victory, when the
Canaanite city-state system was certainly in a state of decline, as
afterwards. Moreover, the references to a number of Israelite tribes
as active participants under Gideon belong to a later stage of

development of the tradition. It is true that that particular development presupposes historical conditions later than those which obtained
at the time of the Song of Deborah, but Gideon's battle itself is not so
easily dated in this way. Finally, it is not so evident that the
expansion of Ammon to come into conflict with Gilead could have
happened only after the decline of Moab. The Ammonites were
settled north-east of Moab, and Ammonite expansion against Gilead
could have taken place quite independently of any contact between
Moab and Benjamin in the area immediately north of the Dead Sea.

There must, indeed, be some reason for the order in which the
stories actually appear in the book of Judges, but if this order is not to
be accounted for by the process of literary growth of the book, it may
well owe much to the geographical location of the events and those
who participated in them. Such an explanation can include also
traditions secondarily attached to the old collection of deliverer
stories: so the setting of the Othniel story is Judah; that of the Ehud
tradition is Benjamin; Deborah came from Ephraim; Gideon's home
was the Manassite clan of Abiezer; Jephthah's victory is set in
Transjordan; and the editors responsible for introducing the Samson
story may have assumed Dan's location in the far north. Thus, the
stories follow a rough south–north sequence.

The relative chronology of events is, therefore, quite uncertain;
but it is still possible to maintain one fixed point with some
assurance. This is the defeat of Sisera by Deborah and Barak,
commemorated in Judg. 4f. Some extremely speculative attempts
have been made to date this event, often by indirect appeal to
archaeological evidence. Thus, Judg. 5.19 has been held to presuppose
that at the time of the battle Megiddo was unoccupied; and such a
break in occupation has been dated between 1150 and 1075 BC. The
battle has, therefore, been fixed at c. 1125 BC. However, this
argument is clearly completely unreliable, and its fallacious nature is
indicated by the fact that it has also been held (by Aharoni) that the
battle could only have taken place when both Taanach and Megiddo
were still strong Canaanite cities. Others have attempted to exploit
the reference in Judg. 5.6 to Shamgar, who, according to Judg. 3.31,
killed six hundred Philistines. For Aharoni this points to the
destruction of the Philistine garrison at Bethshean, which is dated
archaeologically to the end of the thirteenth century; for Alt, on the
other hand, Shamgar's achievements should be related to the time of
the appearance of the Philistines in the Megiddo region, which may

be put at the time of the decline of Megiddo in the second half of the twelfth century. Shamgar, however, was a Canaanite opposed to the Philistines, and the situation presupposed in the Song of Deborah, in which Canaanites and Philistines (Sisera is often taken as a Philistine name) were allied against Israel, signifies, in Alt's view, a considerable change in the political scene. Such a change could not have taken place before the eleventh century, and so it is to that late time that the victory over Sisera should be dated.

Alt's argument is difficult to maintain, but his conclusion is probably correct. One must admit that in a segmentary society of the form constituted by Israel at this time there would have been no uniform development and extension of alliances among the tribes, so that one could say that a wide alliance such as that represented in this event must be later than other events in which no such alliance appears; however, it is still true that the Song of Deborah and the event it commemorates presuppose a developed national consciousness, and self-identification as the people of Yahweh, which could have appeared surely not long before the time when a very similar if not identical group of tribes inaugurated the Israelite monarchy under Saul. The area over which Saul reigned, described in 2 Sam. 2.9, is almost exactly that from which contingents came, or were expected to come, to the help of Deborah and Barak against Sisera.

Furthermore, if it is true that Sisera belonged to the Sea Peoples, of whom the Philistines were also a part, then it is likely that this victory of Israel, which was effectively then a defeat of the Philistines and which left tribal Israel in control of the strategically important plain of Jezreel, would not for long have gone without a Philistine reaction. Just such a reaction appears first in the Philistine defeat of Israel at Aphek recorded in 1 Sam. 4, an event which introduced the conditions at the end of the period of the judges, out of which the monarchy of Saul emerged. Thus, the victory over Sisera was a major step in Israel's realization of its political power, on the way to its assumption of control in Palestine.

### b. From tribal society to monarchic state

It must by now be abundantly clear that it is a distortion of the nature of Israel in the pre-monarchic period to think of it in terms of a society steadily progressing towards the establishment of the monarchy. The fact that it is impossible to establish a chronology of the period of the judges, which means that the stories of the book of Judges take on the appearance of a series of vignettes of Israel rather than a history of Israel, is symptomatic of the situation. Thus, to conclude this account with a section under the title given above can be done only tentatively and with considerable qualification. However, in the end Israel did introduce the monarchic institution, and one is entitled to search for possible roots for this change in the nature of pre-monarchic Israelite society. External factors, such as the threat posed by Ammonites and Philistines, were the immediate cause of the institution of the monarchy, but it is unlikely that any king would ever have been appointed unless some basis for the type of leadership which he represented already existed in Israelite society.

The two instances (apart from the brief references in Judg. 17.6; 18.1; 19.1; 21.25) in which the topic of kingship in Israel features in the book of Judges are not of much relevance here. Abimelech's kingship in Shechem (Judg. 9) was an attempt to revive a form of city-state monarchy and extend it as widely as possible into tribal areas. It had no tribal basis and cannot be held to represent a tendency towards monarchism within tribal Israel. As far as the development of Israelite monarchy is concerned, Abimelech's kingship was probably a quite irrelevant episode. The other apparent reference to kingship is in the Gideon story: in Judg. 8.22f., the men of Israel offer dynastic rule over Israel to Gideon because of his victory over the Midianites, an offer refused by Gideon with the comment that it is Yahweh who rules over Israel. Here at first it seems that a positive indication of monarchic tendencies in Israel is present. However, the passage is clearly not part of the basic Gideon tradition. The latter was concerned with Gideon's leadership of a band of Abiezrites; here it is the 'men of Israel' who offer rule over Israel to Gideon. The passage presupposes a united Israel with single leadership in war; and it surely also presupposes a knowledge of dynastic rule. It is unlikely that this element of the tradition can be dated before the time of David.

In fact, as Crüsemann has shown, Judg. 8.22f. relate very well to David, and are intended to present Gideon as a positive corrective to David. The offer of rule to Gideon and its rejection are immediately followed by the story of his making a golden ephod. This belonged originally with Gideon's reaction to the offer of rulership, as a statement of how Yahweh rules over his people: it is through the ephod that divine direction comes. The ephod was still of great significance in the time of David, and David himself took important political and military decisions only after consulting Yahweh through it (1 Sam. 23.9ff.; 30.6ff.). The offer of dynastic kingship to Gideon and his making of an ephod are an element of the Gideon tradition aimed at the Davidic dynasty; it says in effect that deliverance from enemies, be they Midianites or Philistines, comes under the rule of Yahweh through the ephod, and must not result in the deliverer, Gideon or David, replacing Yahweh as ruler of Israel. It is to the time of David, not that of pre-monarchic Israel, that the tradition of the offer of rule to Gideon belongs.

There was no historical inevitability about the monarchy in Israel in the sense of its being the result of central movements and tendencies in Israel in the period of the judges. It is not surprising, therefore, that Flanagan has proposed a modification to the normal view of the early monarchic period, in order to see it, rather than the period of the judges, as the time of transition between tribal Israel and the monarchic state. So, Saul and David are held to have been leaders of an Israelite society organized as a chiefdom rather than as a monarchic state. A chiefdom is characterized by competition for leadership and by the lack of strict social stratification and of strong centralization, both of which are typical of a monarchic state. A chiefdom is a theocratic society in which the priesthood is prominent; it also has a ranking system (at least, compared with the egalitarianism of a segmentary society), in that those closely related to the chief, who organizes the redistribution of produce, have the status of nobility. So it was in the period between the loss of the ark to the Philistines (1 Sam. 4) and the accession of Solomon that Israel went through the transition from a segmentary society to a monarchic state. This view of the time of the early monarchy certainly fits with the situation presupposed also by the tradition of the offer of dynastic rule to Gideon, studied above; it was a time of transition when a new system had not yet stabilized in the segmentary society of Israel.

This modification in our understanding of the nature of the early monarchy conforms perfectly with the picture of the essential nature of tribal society which has emerged here: it is no transitional phenomenon; rather, it is an independent social structure. Tribalism has indeed been described as 'an evolutionary cul-de-sac'; it did not contain within itself the seeds of development into a centralized monarchic state. In fact, tribalism works against rather than towards the formation of a central authority. Its locus of power is at the bottom, the level of family and clan, rather than at the top, the level of the tribe. A hierarchical structure, such as the monarchic state requires, means a complete break with the social, political and economic principles on which tribal society is based.

The rise of Saul, insofar as it conformed with that of the deliverers in the period of the judges, seems to have had a tribal base; it was as a charismatic deliverer from the tribe of Benjamin that Saul appeared. Such occasional deliverers are known from segmentary societies, and their leadership temporarily breaks the tribal barriers. With the passing of the emergency, however, those barriers are re-established and united leadership disappears. Saul's becoming king represented a break with this pattern; but the extent of it should not be exaggerated. He was king in war only, so that it was really on the basis of a continuing emergency that his monarchy was founded. Moreover, ultimately his kingship failed, and a major reason for the fact that his dynasty did not endure must be that it had not developed a sufficiently strong following which was independent of its tribal base.

David was different: he had in his favour not only the accepted recognition that a capable leader in war was needed, but also the fact that he was independently strong enough to be free of the constraints imposed by tribal society. David with his own personal army could withstand the pressure exerted by tribalism, and could impose a political system which ran counter to the influences it exerted. Saul had a background in the deliverers of the period of the judges; if David has a root there it is to be found not in the deliverers but in the minor judges, and particularly perhaps in Jephthah. In the minor judges, whose association was with cities rather than tribes, there is a non-tribal judicial system which functions to integrate diverse tribal custom into a more unified procedure. In Jephthah there is also a leader who, at the head of his own military band, supplied a precedent for later efforts to forge Israel into a single monarchic state.

### For Further Reading

### I

On Israel in the period of the judges and its relationship with earlier and later times:

M. Noth, *The History of Israel* (New York: Harper, and London: A. & C. Black, 2nd edn, 1960; reprint London: SCM, 1983), 1-7; S.M. Warner, 'The Judges within the Structure of Early Israel', *HUCA* 47 (1976), 57-74; Warner, 'The Dating of the Period of the Judges', *VT* 28 (1978), 455-63; E. Neufeld, 'The Emergence of a Royal-Urban Society in Ancient Israel', *HUCA* 31 (1960), 31-53; N.K. Gottwald, 'Early Israel and the Canaanite Socio-Economic System', *Palestine in Transition: the Emergence of Ancient Israel* (ed. D.N. Freedman and D.F. Graf; Sheffield: Almond, 1983), 25-37.

## II

On the unity of Israel in the pre-monarchic period:

A. Phillips, 'NEBALAH—a term for serious disorderly and unruly conduct', *VT* 25 (1975), 237-42; C.H.J. de Geus, *The Tribes of Israel* (Assen: van Gorcum, 1976), 1-68, 146-48, 163-64; B. Lindars, 'The Israelite Tribes in Judges', VTS 30 (1979), 95-112; N.K. Gottwald, *The Tribes of Yahweh* (New York: Orbis Books, 1979, and London: SCM, 1980), 318-23.

## III

On segmentary societies:

M. Fortes and E.E. Evans-Pritchard, *African Political Systems* (Oxford: Oxford University Press, 1940); L. Mair, *An Introduction to Social Anthropology* (Oxford: Clarendon Press, [2]1972), 67-82; I.M. Lewis, *Social Anthropology in Perspective* (Harmondsworth: Penguin, 1976), 323-33; for the Israelite context, A. Malamat, 'Tribal Societies: Biblical Genealogies and African Lineage Systems', *Archives Européennes de Sociologie* 14 (1973), 126-36; F. Crüsemann, *Der Widerstand gegen das Königtum* (WMANT, 49; Neukirchen-Vluyn: Neukirchener Verlag, 1978), 201-208; N. Lohfink, 'Die segmentären Gesellschaften Afrikas als neue Analogie für das vorstaatliche Israel', *Bibel und Kirche* 2/2 (1983), 55-58.

## IV

On the historical background of the deliverer stories:

M. Noth, *The History of Israel* (New York: Harper, and London: A. &
C. Black, 2nd edn, 1960; reprint London: SCM, 1983), 141-63; R. de
Vaux, *The Early History of Israel* (London: Darton, Longman and
Todd, and Philadelphia: Westminster Press, 1978), II, 775-824;
A.D.H. Mayes, 'The Period of the Judges', in *Israelite and Judaean
History* (ed. J. Hayes and J.M. Miller; Philadelphia: Westminster
Press, and London: SCM, 1977), 308-22; H. Reviv, 'The Government
of Shechem in the El Amarna Period and in the Days of Abimelech',
*IEJ* 16 (1966), 252-57.

## V

On the holy war and charismatic leadership:

R. Smend, *Yahweh War and Tribal Confederation* (Nashville:
Abingdon, 1970); F. Stolz, *Jahwes und Israels Kriege: Kriegstheorien
und Kriegserfahrungen im Glauben des alten Israel* (ATANT, 60;
Zürich: Theologischer Verlag, 1972); G.H. Jones, '"Holy War" or
"Yahweh War"?', *VT* 25 (1975), 642-58; A. Malamat, 'Charismatic
Leadership in the Book of Judges', *Magnalia Dei. The Mighty Acts of
God. Essays on the Bible and Archaeology in Memory of G.E. Wright*
(ed. F.M. Cross, W.E. Lemke, P.D. Miller; New York: Doubleday,
1976), 152-68.

## VI

On the minor judges:

M. Noth, 'Das Amt des Richters Israels', *Bertholet Festschrift* (ed. W.
Baumgartner, O. Eissfeldt, K. Elliger, L. Rost; Tübingen: J.C.B.
Mohr, 1950), 404-17 (= his *Gesammelte Studien*, II [München:
Kaiser Verlag, 1969], 71-85); W. Richter, 'Zu den "Richtern Israels"',
*ZAW* 67 (1965), 40-72; R. de Vaux, *The Early History of Israel*
(London: Darton, Longman and Todd, and Philadelphia: Westminster
Press, 1978), II, 751-73; H.N. Rösel, 'Die "Richter Israels"', *BZ* 25
(1981), 180-203.

## VII

On the chronology of the period of the judges:

A. Malamat, 'The War of Gideon and Midian. A Military Approach',

*PEQ* 85 (1953), 61-65; Malamat, 'The Period of the Judges', *World History of the Jewish People*, I/3 (ed. B. Mazar; London: W.H. Allen, 1971), 129-63; Malamat, 'Charismatic Leadership in the Book of Judges', *Magnalia Dei* (ed. F.M. Cross, W.E. Lemke, P.D. Miller; New York: Doubleday, 1976), 152-68; A. Alt, 'Megiddo im Übergang vom kanaanäischen zum israelitischen Zeitalter', *ZAW* 62 (1944), 67-85 (= his *Kleine Schriften*, I [München: C.H. Beck'sche Verlagsbuchhandlung, 1953], 256-73); Y. Aharoni, 'New Aspects of the Israelite Occupation of the North', *Near Eastern Archaeology in the Twentieth Century. Essays in Honor of Nelson Glueck* (ed. J.A. Sanders; New York: Doubleday, 1970), 254-67; A.D.H. Mayes, *Israel in the Period of the Judges* (London: SCM, and Naperville: A.R. Allenson, 1974), 92-98.

## VIII

On the pre-monarchic roots of Israelite kingship:

C.H.J. de Geus, *The Tribes of Israel* (Assen: van Gorcum, 1976), 130-32, 204-207; F. Crüsemann, *Der Widerstand gegen das Königtum* (WMANT, 49; Neukirchen-Vluyn: Neukirchener Verlag, 1978), 42-54; J.W. Flanagan, 'Chiefs in Israel', *JSOT* 20 (1981), 47-73.

# INDEXES

## INDEX OF BIBLICAL REFERENCES

# INDEX OF SUBJECTS

# INDEX OF AUTHORS

Round and round the past I go
Round and round my mind I go
How could he . . . ?
Why couldn't I . . . ?
Go on, though the tension in my mind winds
like a bobbin, set tight, thread pulling
arm rising, falling. Will it snap?
Will it hold?

                         I thought he told me I'm The One
                           But how is one plus one
                          not two, but just plain one
                        and one, and this One
                        neither all nor only
                  to him in whom I saw the ocean
                        and myself a drop,
                              Broken in half,
                              Lost in his surf?

Round and round the future I go
Round and round my mind I go
Who will he . . . ?
How will I
go on?, when the tension in my mind winds
like a bobbin, set tight, thread pulling
arm rising, falling

Ris**ing**, **fa**lling;
Will it snap? Will it hold?